The Love of God Holds Creation Together

Monographs in Baptist History

VOLUME 7

SERIES EDITOR
Michael A. G. Haykin, The Southern Baptist Theological Seminary

EDITORIAL BOARD
Matthew Barrett, Midwestern Baptist Theological Seminary
Peter Beck, Charleston Southern University
Anthony L. Chute, California Baptist University
Jason G. Duesing, Midwest Baptist Theological Seminary
Nathan A. Finn, Union University
Crawford Gribben, Queen's University, Belfast
Gordon L. Heath, McMaster Divinity College
Barry Howson, Heritage Theological Seminary
Jason K. Lee, Cedarville University
Thomas J. Nettles, The Southern Baptist Theological Seminary, retired
James A. Patterson, Union University
James M. Renihan, Institute of Reformed Baptist Studies
Jeffrey P. Straub, Central Seminary
Brian R. Talbot, Broughty Ferry Baptist Church, Scotland
Malcolm B. Yarnell III, Southwestern Baptist Theological Seminary

Ours is a day in which not only the gaze of western culture but also increasingly that of Evangelicals is riveted to the present. The past seems to be nowhere in view and hence it is disparagingly dismissed as being of little value for our rapidly changing world. Such historical amnesia is fatal for any culture, but particularly so for Christian communities whose identity is profoundly bound up with their history. The goal of this new series of monographs, Studies in Baptist History, seeks to provide one of these Christian communities, that of evangelical Baptists, with reasons and resources for remembering the past. The editors are deeply convinced that Baptist history contains rich resources of theological reflection, praxis and spirituality that can help Baptists, as well as other Christians, live more Christianly in the present. The monographs in this series will therefore aim at illuminating various aspects of the Baptist tradition and in the process provide Baptists with a usable past.

The Love of God Holds Creation Together

Andrew Fuller's Theology of Virtue

Ryan P. Hoselton

FOREWORD BY
Michael A. G. Haykin

☙PICKWICK *Publications* · Eugene, Oregon

THE LOVE OF GOD HOLDS CREATION TOGETHER
Andrew Fuller's Theology of Virtue

Monographs in Baptist History 7

Copyright © 2018 Ryan P. Hoselton. All rights reserved. Except for brief quotations in critical publications or reviews, no part of this book may be reproduced in any manner without prior written permission from the publisher. Write: Permissions, Wipf and Stock Publishers, 199 W. 8th Ave., Suite 3, Eugene, OR 97401.

Pickwick Publications
An Imprint of Wipf and Stock Publishers
199 W. 8th Ave., Suite 3
Eugene, OR 97401

www.wipfandstock.com

PAPERBACK ISBN: 978-1-5326-1858-1
HARDCOVER ISBN: 978-1-4982-4428-2
EBOOK ISBN: 978-1-4982-4427-5

Cataloguing-in-Publication data:

Names: Hoselton, Ryan P.

Title: The love of God holds creation together : Andrew Fuller's theology of virtue / by Ryan P. Hoselton; foreword by Micahel A. G. Haykin.

Description: Eugene, OR: Pickwick Publications, 2018 | Monographs in Baptist History 7 | Includes bibliographical references and index.

Identifiers: ISBN 978-1-5326-1858-1 (paperback) | ISBN 978-1-4982-4428-2 (hardcover) | ISBN 978-1-4982-4427-5 (ebook)

Subjects: LCSH: Fuller, Andrew, 1754–1815. | Virtue. | God (Christianity)—Love. | Baptists—Doctrines.

Classification: BX6495.F75 H67 2018 (print) | BX6495.F75 (ebook)

Manufactured in the U.S.A.   02/20/18

For Jaclyn.

May the love of God hold us together always.

Contents

Foreword by Michael A. G. Haykin | ix
Preface | xi
Abbreviations | xii

1. Introduction | 1
2. "The Power of Sinful Men": Fuller and Moral Inability | 5
3. "Religion that Inspires the Love of God": Fuller's Aretegenic Orthodoxy | 25
4. "A System of Holiness": Fuller's Evangelical Calvinistic Theology of Virtue | 47
5. "Abide in the Vine": The Source and Motivation of Virtue | 69
6. Conclusion | 88

Bibliography | 93
Name Index | 99
Subject Index | 103

Foreword

It never ceases to amaze me that even good historians can all too frequently ask questions of historical documents and eras that reflect more their own concerns and context than the people and periods that they are studying. The theology of Andrew Fuller, the remarkable eighteenth-century pastor-theologian, is an excellent case in point. In the past fifty years or so, the questions posed by historians of his published corpus have centered around issues primarily related to soteriology, and especially the whole matter of the free offer of the gospel and cross-cultural mission, matters of concern to contemporary Christianity. To be sure, these areas were central to the world of Fuller and his circle of friends, and he wrote a groundbreaking work about them, namely, *The Gospel Worthy of All Acceptation*. But what has not been recognized by scholarly discussion of Fuller and his thought, for instance, is his great interest in ethics, and especially the whole matter of virtue, an area of thought that has languished to some degree in the world of Evangelical academe. In this regard, then, this small work by Ryan Hoselton, which originated as a master's thesis, truly does what we hope all post-baccalaureate theses will do, and that is break new ground.

Hoselton shows how vital the whole concept of love was for Fuller's thinking and action. And in this Fuller is showing his deep indebtedness to his main theological mentor after the Bible, namely Jonathan Edwards. Of course, once the centrality of love for Fuller is demonstrated, as it is in this essay, students of Fuller will recall how this theme was there all along. What was it, for example, that so struck Fuller about his close friend Samuel Pearce, the seraphic preacher of industrial Birmingham—was it not his "holy love"?

Foreword

It is a delight to introduce this fine study of a truly vital area of Fuller's thinking, and pray that it will be the launching point for more studies of the concept of virtue in the most important Baptist author of the transatlantic world in the latter decades of the long eighteenth century.

Michael A. G. Haykin

Dundas, Ontario
March 29, 2017

Preface

I WISH TO EXPRESS my deep appreciation to Professor Michael A. G. Haykin, not only for giving me the opportunity to write this book, which began as a master's thesis at the Southern Baptist Theological Seminary, but also for his constructive feedback, encouragement, and patience throughout the process. I was immediately interested in this project when he mentioned that so little has been done on Baptist ethical thought. Professors Gregory Wills and Paul Helm served on my committee and offered invaluable insight and support, for which I'm sincerely grateful. Roy Paul also deserves credit and my hearty appreciation for assisting with the indexes. About eleven years ago, Thomas Dollahite, a close friend from New Mexico, had introduced me not only to Baptist history and theology, but also to my Savior. My ambition and prayer is to bless others in the same way that he has blessed me. My wife Jaclyn gave birth to our first daughter, Madrid Idelette, between chapters 1 and 2. A decent portion of this book was written with one hand while the other was fixing her pacifier or clenched by her superhuman grip. I thank Jaclyn for her care and support, lovingly bearing with me on the evenings that I transitioned straight from work to my study. I look forward to many years of growing our family in the knowledge and love of God.

Ryan P. Hoselton

Heidelberg, Germany
March 2017

Abbreviations

WAF *The Complete Works of the Rev. Andrew Fuller with a Memoir of His Life* by Andrew Gunton Fuller

WJE *The Works of Jonathan Edwards*

1

Introduction

THE RISE IN ATTENTION to Andrew Fuller (1754–1815) is long overdue. In the early nineteenth century, the historian Joseph Ivimey (1773–1834) envisioned that Fuller would "be remembered with esteem and veneration by all who feel an interest for the salvation of the heathen and the prosperity of the denomination."[1] Recent scholarly and ministerial initiatives have labored to bring Ivimey's desire to fruition. According to Michael Haykin, the Director of the Andrew Fuller Center for Baptist Studies, interest in Fuller's life and thought is "currently undergoing a small renaissance."[2] Historians and theologians alike are rediscovering Fuller's role in shaping not only Baptist identity[3] but also transatlantic Evangelicalism,[4] while many pastors are commending Fuller as an example for ministers today.[5]

Most treatments of Fuller's life and thought have underlined his Evangelical Calvinist soteriology and missiology.[6] Fuller's articulation of Evan-

---

1. Ivimey, *History of the English Baptists*, 4:535.

2. Haykin, in preface of Brewster, *Andrew Fuller*, xv. The Andrew Fuller Center for Baptist Studies, located at the Southern Baptist Theological Seminary in Louisville, Kentucky, hosts annual conferences on Andrew Fuller, a web-blog, and *The Andrew Fuller Center Review*.

3. For works that treat Fuller's role in Baptist life, see Nettles, *By His Grace*, 108–30; Roberts, "Andrew Fuller," 121–39; Haykin, "Particular Redemption," 122–38; Nuttall, "Northamptonshire and the Modern Question," 101–23.

4. For works that address Fuller's role in Evangelicalism, see Bebbington, *Evangelicalism in Modern Britain*, 63–65; Noll, *Rise of Evangelicalism*, 207–9; Sweeney, *Nathaniel Taylor*, 124; Watts, *Dissenters*, 458–64.

5. Brewster, *Andrew Fuller*; Piper, *Andrew Fuller*.

6. Many dissertations on Fuller demonstrate an occupation with these themes: Kirby,

gelical Calvinism perceived a direct relationship between God's sovereignty and evangelistic tenacity, laying the ideological framework for the modern missionary movement. Without question, Fuller's advocacy of Evangelical Calvinist thought and practice—which eventually became known as Fullerism—remains his greatest contribution to the early Evangelical movement. Peter Morden's intellectual biography of Fuller represents how most historians and pastors have perceived him: the quintessential Evangelical.[7] Morden presents Fuller through the grid of David Bebbington's well-known quadrilateral of Evangelical identity: conversionism, activism, biblicism, and crucicentrism.[8] According to Bebbington, Fuller based his Evangelical Calvinism on Jonathan Edwards's Enlightenment reinterpretation of the relationship between God's sovereignty and human responsibility as "an expression of the law of cause and effect."[9] Therefore, deduces Bebbington, Fuller's reliance on Edwards "was sufficient to ensure" that the Evangelical movement was "built on Enlightenment foundations."[10]

This book focuses on an area of Fuller's thought that directly undermined Enlightenment foundations: ethics. Fuller countered the verdict of many Enlightenment thinkers that traditional Christian belief was deleterious to moral excellence. He defended the veracity of censured orthodox doctrines—such as the Trinity, the atonement, human depravity, and the truth of Scripture—on the basis that they were conducive to virtue, human flourishing, and happiness. His apologetic method perpetuated a treasured idea of pre-modern theologians like Augustine of Hippo (354–430) and John Calvin (1509–1564)—that the truth and essence of orthodoxy consists not merely in its factuality but also its goodness. Like many of the classic theologians, Fuller rooted morality in right Christian doctrine. A

"Theology of Andrew Fuller"; Oliver, "Emergence of a Strict and Particular Baptist Community"; Ascol, "Doctrines of Grace"; Box, "Atonement in the Thought of Andrew Fuller"; Young, "Place of Andrew Fuller"; Mauldin, *Fullerism as Opposed to Calvinism*.

7. Morden, *Offering Christ to the World*. Morden has recently written a more comprehensive biography on Fuller. However, as he admits, there are gaps in his treatment. Wishing to highlight "what made him tick," he leaves out any analysis of Fuller's work, *Gospel Its Own Witness*, and consequently he devotes little attention to Fuller's understanding of virtue. I don't wish to argue that Fuller's theology of virtue was the driving force behind his thought and ministry, but it was certainly a theme that pervaded his corpus and buttressed the most central aspects of his thinking. Morden, *Life and Thought of Andrew Fuller*, 8-9.

8. Bebbington, *Evangelicalism in Modern Britain*, 3.

9. Ibid., 64.

10. Ibid., 65.

right knowledge of God and human nature grounded a correct knowledge of virtue, and a vital love of God and neighbor facilitated a love of virtue. Thus, Fuller's Evangelical Calvinism shaped more than his zealous conversionism; it provided the foundation and motivation of virtue and determined humanity's moral *telos*.

Extremely helpful in examining Fuller's theology of virtue is a work by Ellen Charry on virtue and theology. Her interpretation of the motive behind classic theologians through the centuries, who guarded and promoted Christian orthodoxy because it facilitated virtue and human excellence, applies aptly to Andrew Fuller. Charry offers the neologism "aretegenic" to capture the "virtue-shaping function of the divine pedagogy of theological treatises."[11] The adjective "aretegenic" ("aretology" in its nominal form) is a compound of the Greek terms, *aretē*, denoting "virtue," and *gennaō*, "to beget." The classic theologians believed that an accurate knowledge of God was aretegenic—it fostered virtue and excellence in the lives of believers. Examining theological texts spanning from the New Testament to the Reformation, Charry's project aims at "reclaiming a genuine pastoral Christian psychology that grounds human excellence in knowing and loving God."[12] This book seeks to contribute to this objective by studying the aretegenic theology of Andrew Fuller's Evangelical Calvinism.

Fuller developed his theology of goodness most extensively in his polemical works against Socinianism, *The Calvinistic and Socinian Systems Examined and Compared, as to Their Moral Tendency* (1793, 1802), and Deism, *The Gospel Its Own Witness* (1800). Thus, the material from these treatises will furnish most of the body of this book. He composed these works in response to the writings of Joseph Priestley (1733–1804) and Thomas Paine (1737–1809), two of the most widely known eighteenth-century critics of orthodox belief. Although Priestley and Paine were very different figures in many respects, they both rested a substantial portion of their diatribe against orthodoxy on the basis of its inherent proclivity to immorality—a contention that Fuller deemed unfounded.

Chapter 2 focuses on the formation of Fuller's Evangelical Calvinist thought early in his ministry career and the role it played in establishing his theology of virtue. Also, while a thorough treatment of Fuller's Enlightenment context is not within the bounds of this book, a brief analysis of its moral philosophy, as well as the views of Priestley and Paine, is necessary

---

11. Charry, *Renewing of Your Minds*, 19.
12. Ibid., 18.

in order to understand Fuller's attempt to challenge its moral foundations. His understanding of humanity's moral inability contrasted sharply with the modernist anthropology, necessitating Evangelical truth to return men and women from their moral rebellion against God. Chapter 3 introduces the background and design of his polemical works against Socinianism and Deism. This chapter shows how Fuller's understanding of Christian orthodoxy as aretegenic grounded his apology in both debates. Chapter 4 presents a systematic analysis of how Fuller's Evangelical Calvinist doctrine provided the framework for his theology of virtue. Fuller aimed to re-enchant moral reasoning by situating it in a cosmic theological drama in which the righteous and loving Moral Governor provides a way to pardon immoral rebels. Chapter 5 examines how, according to Fuller, Evangelical Calvinist doctrine motivates virtue, love, and happiness in the lives of Christians and contributes to the welfare of others. He maintained that the Enlightenment confidence in love of self to inspire virtue failed in comparison to making the love of God one's ultimate end. Chapter 6 concludes with a brief analysis of how Fuller's theology of virtue relates to virtue ethics today, demonstrating how his critique of Enlightenment moral foundations parallels that of some ethicists like Alisdair MacIntyre.

In search of a universal standard of morality, many Enlightenment thinkers replaced religion with the self as normative for morality. MacIntyre and others have argued that this shift ironically lent itself to emotivism and individualist ethics, which Fuller identified in bolder terms as self-idolatry and moral rebellion against what God has established for mankind's moral teleology. For Fuller, the human self with its conflicting ethical inclinations lacked the moral ability to cultivate true virtue. Mankind needed the knowledge and love of God through the person and atoning work of Jesus Christ—for if you know Christ, "Ye shall know the truth, and the truth shall make you free."[13]

---

13. Fuller, *Calvinistic and Socinian Systems Examined*, in WAF, 2:163. Fuller cited John 8:32.

2

"The Power of Sinful Men": Fuller and Moral Inability

ANDREW FULLER'S SOCIAL AND religious context was instrumental in shaping his ethical thought.[1] The debates and questions that he faced as an eighteenth-century British Particular Baptist forced him to work out his own understanding of human moral accountability before God. As a Baptist, he did not have access to many of the same educational and social influences as many of his Anglican or Presbyterian contemporaries—his primary influences came from his self-initiated study of past theologians. His education and background heavily informed his conviction that true virtue must be grounded in Christian orthodox belief, and he developed this view most thoroughly in his treatises defending Christianity against the Socinians and Deists. For Radical Enlightenment figures like Joseph Priestley and Thomas Paine, human nature had great potential for moral good. Fuller aimed to challenge this claim, insisting that men and women had no inherent moral ability to attain virtue and desperately needed the gospel.

Fuller's Life and the Shaping of His Thought

Andrew Fuller was born on February 6, 1754, to Robert Fuller (d. 1781) and Philippa Gunton (d. 1816) in Wicken, a village in Cambridgeshire, England.[2] The Fullers moved to Soham in 1761, where they raised Andrew

---

1. The quote in the chapter title is from Ryland, *Life and Death of the Rev. Andrew Fuller*, 13–15.

2. For recent biographical works on Fuller, see Morden, "Andrew Fuller," 1–42,

to assist with the small family farm. His heritage on both sides of the family was thoroughly Non-Conformist, marked with the scars of the social marginalization they endured through the strenuous seventeenth century.[3] The Fullers attended the Particular Baptist church at Soham—where Andrew's maternal grandmother had her membership since its founding.[4] The community surrounding this congregation set the stage for the early formation of Fuller's ministry career and thought.

> My father and mother were Dissenters, of the Calvinistic persuasion, who were in the habit of hearing Mr. Eve, a Baptist minister, who being what is here termed *high* in his sentiments, or tinged with false Calvinism, had little or nothing to say to the unconverted. I therefore never considered myself as any way concerned in what I heard from the pulpit. Nevertheless by reading and reflection I was sometimes strongly impressed in a way of conviction. My parents were engaged in husbandry, which occupation therefore, I followed to the twentieth year of my age. I remember many of the sins of my childhood, among which were lying, cursing, and swearing.... I think I must have been nearly fourteen years old, before I began to think about futurity. The preaching upon which I attended was not adapted to awaken my conscience, as the minister had seldom any thing to say except to believers, and what believing was I neither knew, nor was greatly concerned to know.... I satisfied myself thinking it was not of immediate concern, and I should understand it as I grew older. ... I was at times the subject of such convictions and affections,

---

Offering Christ to the World, and *Life and Thought of Andrew Fuller*; Brewster, *Andrew Fuller*; and Roberts, "Andrew Fuller," 34–51. Haykin's biography of John Sutcliff includes a chapter on Fuller, and the work provides valuable and detailed historical insight into his circle of friends and the Particular Baptist context. Haykin, *One Heart and One Soul*. For more on Fuller's life and piety from his personal letters, see Haykin, *Armies of the Lamb*.

Prominent nineteenth-century biographies on Fuller include Ryland, *Life and Death of the Rev. Andrew Fuller*; and A. G. Fuller, Memoir, in *WAF*, 1:1–116; and *Men Worth Remembering*. Ryland had the most access to the primary resources and was of kindred sentiments with Fuller, thus I rely most heavily on his account. My book mainly uses Ryland's 1816 edition.

For a succinct treatment of Fuller's life and thought, see Clipsham, "Andrew Fuller and Fullerism," 99–114. Clipsham introduces the reader to Fuller's biographical information, Fullerism, his contest against Hyper-Calvinists, influence on the missionary movement, evangelical Calvinism, pastoral work, church affairs, the impact of Edwards on his theology and practice, and his network of friendships.

3. Ryland, *Life and Death of the Rev. Andrew Fuller*, 13–15.

4. Ibid., 14.

that I really thought myself converted; and lived under that delusion for a long time.[5]

Fuller's occasional raptures of religious passion mixed with his recurrent waywardness—like when he "engaged in games of hazard" and "idle tricks"—provoked agonizing uncertainty in Fuller over the state of his salvation through his early-mid teenage years.[6] "I was not then aware," Fuller reflected, "that any poor sinner had a warrant to believe in Christ for the salvation of his soul; but supposed there must be some kind of qualification to entitle him to do it."[7] It was not until November 1769 when he admitted that he "had no qualifications" that he rested faith in Christ. "I will trust my soul—my sinful, lost soul in his hands. If I perish, I perish. However it was, I was determined to cast myself upon Christ . . . [and] my guilt and fears were gradually and insensibly removed."[8] The following March, at sixteen years of age, Fuller was baptized and became a member of the Baptist church at Soham.[9]

Fuller perceived a direct relationship between his conversion experience and his personal morality. Wrong thinking and doing was still present in his life as a Christian—a reality he readily acknowledged. Looking back on the events surrounding his baptism, he recalled how his heart filled with resentful hate when a "company of young men" mocked him for "having been dipped."[10] He also remembered the temptation to entertain youthful sensual urges. However, upon his conversion, he gradually learned to resist wrongdoing by turning to God in faith and prayer. His new knowledge and love of God provided him with the motivation to aspire to virtue and find joy in imitating his Lord's ways rather than in wrongdoing.

In the autumn of 1769, Fuller confronted a man in his congregation who refused to repent and reform his drunkenness. Despite Fuller's imploring to turn from his sin, the man responded that he was not capable of changing his behavior. The pastor, John Eve (d. 1782), supported Fuller, a move that ignited a divisive controversy in the congregation. According to Fuller, the whole affair pertained to "the power of sinful men to do the

---

5. Quoted in ibid., 17–21. Fuller wrote these reflections in a letter in 1798.
6. Ibid., 24.
7. Ibid., 29.
8. Ibid., 29–30.
9. Ibid., 35.
10. Ibid., 35.

will of God, and to keep themselves from sin."[11] The congregation's position on human ability to pursue moral excellence was rooted in their high Calvinist answer to the Modern Question—one of the most heated issues in eighteenth-century Baptist circles.[12] The Modern Question asked whether all of humanity has the duty to obey God's commands, one of which was to believe the gospel. High Calvinists reasoned that since Christ died exclusively for the elect, only the chosen have the power to respond to God's commands in faith and obedience. They deduced that those who do not possess the ability do not have the duty, rendering it absurd for ministers to call unbelievers to follow Christ in faith and righteous living.

Fuller initially understood that everyone had the obligation to follow God's commands, but he was persuaded to change his mind and side with the congregation against Eve, whose Calvinism apparently did not reach high enough. In 1775, after Eve's dismissal, the church called Fuller to fill his place as their minister. He accepted the offer, but he was not fully satisfied with the high Calvinist logic on the Modern Question, "I perceived that some kind of power was necessary to render us accountable beings."[13] Early in Fuller's pastorate, he grew close with a group of Particular Baptist leaders who played an instrumental role in the development of his thought and ministry.[14] At Fuller's ordination service in spring 1775, Robert Hall Sr. (1728–1791), the pastor of Arnesby Baptist Church, commended "Edwards on the Will" to help settle his conflict.[15] "Not being much acquainted with

---

11. Ibid., 38.

12. Nuttall, "Northamptonshire and the Modern Question," 208–9.

13. Quoted in Ryland, *Life and Death of the Rev. Andrew Fuller*, 40.

14. For more on this friendship dynamic, see Clipsham, "Andrew Fuller and Fullerism," 217. An entire conference was devoted to this theme entitled "Andrew Fuller and his Friends" at the Andrew Fuller Center for Baptist Studies, in Louisville on September 21–22, 2012.

15. Quoted in Ryland, *Life and Death of the Rev. Andrew Fuller*, 58. Like most non-wealthy Non-Conformists, Fuller had no formal education. Baptists were not allowed in most English universities. It is a remarkable feat, in light of his background, that Fuller's late start on his self-education earned him honorary doctorates from both Yale University and the College of New Jersey (both of which he declined in order to avoid hierarchical distinctions among his Baptist brothers). Timothy Dwight, president of Yale University and the grandson of Jonathan Edwards, wrote to Fuller, "This act is the result of the knowledge of your personal character and your published works." See A. G. Fuller, *Memoir*, in *WAF*, 1:84–85.

For a work on Edwards's impact on the Baptist community, see Haykin, "Great Admirers," 197–207. Haykin writes, "Andrew Fuller appears to have been the main conduit by which the ideas of Edwards and his New Divinity followers made their way into Baptist

books at that time," Fuller initially confused Jonathan Edwards (1703–1758) of New England with John Edwards (1637–1716) of Cambridge. When he read the latter's work, *Veritas Redux*, he was naturally puzzled why Hall referred it to him.

Fuller then came across a pamphlet by Abraham Taylor entitled *The Modern Question*. Although initially unimpressed with "his reasonings," Fuller could not deny his point that "the addresses of John the Baptist, Christ, and the Apostles" enjoined repentance and faith from "the ungodly."[16] As a committed biblicist, determined "to take up no principle at second-hand; but to search for every thing at the pure fountain of thy word," Taylor's argument from Scripture won him over.[17] However, his mind remained unsettled on the question of moral accountability. He surveyed the standard Baptist theologians—John Bunyan (1628–1688), John Gill (1697–1771), and John Brine (1703–1765)—but he found no resolution to his dilemma. In 1777, Fuller finally realized his error in reading the wrong Edwards and quickly digested the *Freedom of the Will*, initiating a lifelong study of the New England theologian.[18]

In reading Edwards, Fuller found his answer to the Modern Question, and the implications he drew from this study largely shaped the Evangelical Calvinist theology that he set against not only High Calvinism but also Arminianism, Antinomianism, Sandemanianism, and the two ideologies most pertinent to this study: Deism and Socinianism.[19] Jonathan Edwards wrote *Freedom of the Will* in 1754—the same year that Fuller was born—as a polemical work against the Arminian understanding of human agency.[20] As the full title suggests, the subject matter of human will had strong ethical implications for Edwards: *A Careful and Strict Inquiry into the Modern Prevailing Notions of that Freedom of Will, Which is Supposed to be Essential to Moral Agency, Virtue and Vice, Reward and Punishment, Praise and Blame*. The same would be true for Fuller.

---

life and thought." Haykin, "Great Admirers," 206.

16. Quoted in Ryland, *Life and Death of the Rev. Andrew Fuller*, 60.

17. Ibid., 203.

18. Ibid., 58–59. For a work that details the impact of Jonathan Edwards's thought on Fuller, see Chun, *Legacy of Jonathan Edwards*.

19. For a work on Fuller's engagement with these ideologies, see Haykin, *"At the Pure Fountain of Thy Word"*.

20. Edwards, *Freedom of the Will*.

The Love of God Holds Creation Together

The argument that impacted Fuller most was Edwards's distinction between natural and moral inability. According to both the high Calvinist and Arminian schemes, God would be unfair to make demands that the unregenerate were incapable of performing. Edwards accepted this axiom, but he reconciled it with the idea that God also required universal obedience. The key to understanding God's sovereign fairness in issuing commands that moral agents could not perform rested in properly differentiating between man's natural and moral inability.

> The nature of moral inability, as distinguished from natural: where it was observed, that a man may be said to be morally unable to do a thing, when he is under the influence or prevalence of a contrary inclination, or has a want of inclination . . . [the] will is always, and in every individual act, necessarily determined by the strongest motive; and so is always unable to go against the motive.[21]

For Edwards, if disobedience was due to the agent's incapacitated natural faculties or an "external hindrance"—like an obstruction that prevented learning God's decrees—then God could not justly hold him or her accountable.[22] But since "the will itself" and not human natural faculties "is the proper object of precept or command," God was entirely just in both commanding all moral agents to obedience and in punishing them for disobedience.[23] Every moral agent chose according to his or her most dominant inclination, and everyone's inclination resiliently resisted God's commands. Even if everyone had all access to and understanding of God's moral decrees, all would still disobey because the human moral will is inclined toward wickedness. Thus, as Chris Chun notes, Edwards believed that "every instance of disobedience is one of moral inability."[24]

Having "found much satisfaction" in Edwards's distinction between natural and moral inability as the best explanation of human accountability, Fuller situated its logic at the hinge of his own response to the Modern Question in his watershed work, *The Gospel Worthy of All Acceptation* (1785).[25]

> If it were not the duty of unconverted sinners to believe in Christ, and that because of their inability, he [Fuller speaking in third

---

21. Ibid., 305.
22. Ibid., 309.
23. Ibid., 302.
24. Chun, *Legacy of Jonathan Edwards*, 24.
25. Fuller, *Gospel Worthy of All Acceptation*, in *WAF*, 2:328–416.

person] supposed this inability must be natural, or something which did not arise from an evil disposition; but the more he examined the Scriptures, the more he was convinced that all the inability ascribed to man, with respect to believing, arises from the aversion of his heart. They *will not* come to Christ that they may have life . . . and *desire not* the knowledge of his ways.[26]

Edwards's distinction between natural and moral inability enabled Fuller to promote Calvinist theology and indiscriminate gospel preaching hand in hand. Fuller concluded that since everyone possessed the natural ability to come to Christ in faith, God was entirely fair to require obedience and faith from all humanity—even if some did not have access to explicit revelation of his commands. Voluntary commitment to evil was insufficient to excuse the moral agent. Each individual was accountable to his or her choices that arose from personal desire, and for Fuller, to "desire not the knowledge of his ways" was equivalent to a deliberate hostility to the essence of goodness. Since "there still exists a metaphysical and physical possibility of change within the dispositional inclination," it was the duty of every moral agent to believe whatever God prescribed—and he enjoined belief in the gospel.[27] Fuller reasoned that if humanity has the duty to believe in the gospel, ministers had the responsibility to proclaim it. God worked through the preaching of the gospel as his established means to transform an agent's inclination, making him or her able to willfully follow God in faith and learn to practice and cherish righteousness.

Fuller's answer to the Modern Question—although it drew heavy criticism from high Calvinists and Arminians alike[28]—was instrumental in laying the ideological groundwork for the revitalization of Particular Baptist church life and the modern missionary movement.[29] From 1783—when he became the pastor of the influential Baptist Church in Kettering—until his death in 1815, Fuller was an active member of the Northamptonshire Association, traveled all over Britain for preaching engagements, and he inspired a network of likeminded Evangelical Calvinist ministers who advocated indiscriminate gospel offers.[30] In 1792, Fuller co-founded the

26. Ibid., 2:330. Emphasis original.

27. Chun, *Legacy of Jonathan Edwards*, 61.

28. For more on Fuller's controversy with high Calvinists and Arminians over this work, see chapter 3 of Morden, *Offering Christ to the World*, 52–75.

29. For a work that details the relationship between Fullerism and the missionary movement, see Chun, "Mainspring of Missionary Thought," 335–55.

30. For more on Fuller's role as a pastor and his impact on Baptist life in Britain, see

The Love of God Holds Creation Together

Baptist Missionary Society that sent William Carey and his team to India, prompting a transatlantic crusade of Baptist missionaries eager to take salvation to the lost.[31] Fuller's new understanding of the dynamic between a good and sovereign God and immoral humanity catalyzed his life mission and established his legacy in the history of Evangelicalism.

The development that led to the publication of *The Gospel Worthy of All Acceptation* accomplished several things in Fuller's thought: it established the corrupt moral nature of humanity, vindicated the goodness of the Calvinist understanding of God, and it confirmed the value of the doctrines of the gospel in achieving moral excellence. The Evangelical Calvinist system, unlike any other, was able to restore humanity to the love of God and to the imitation of his righteous ways.

Fuller's Evangelical Calvinist ideological framework that answered the Modern Question heavily determined his views on virtue. One of Fuller's letters to John Ryland Jr., dated March 1783, previews the early formation of his ethical thought and displays clear traces from Edwards.

> How comes sin to be the greatest apparent good in the view of the mind? Is it owing to a natural or a moral defect that men call evil good and good evil? If the former, why was Israel blamed for so doing? If the latter, then it is to be imputed, as you say, to the depraved state of the mind, which views things different from what they are.[32]

Fuller discerned a powerful link between one's moral nature and his or her beliefs—each affected the other. The proclivity to follow corrupt inclinations skewed not only the accuracy of one's belief in the truth but also one's love of it. In October 1783, at his installation service for the Baptist Church in Kettering, Fuller further expounded on the dynamic between knowledge and human immorality in Article VII of his *Confession of Faith*.

> I believe that men are now born and grow up with a vile propensity to moral evil, and herein lies their inability to keep God's law, and as such it is a moral and a criminal inability. Were they but of a right disposition of mind there is nothing now in the law of God but what they could perform; but being wholly under the dominion of sin they have no heart remaining for God, but are full

---

Morden, *Offering Christ to the World*, 103–27.

31. Ryland, *Life and Death of the Rev. Andrew Fuller*, 237–52.

32. Andrew Fuller, to John Ryland Jr., March 22, 1783, Typed Fuller's Letters, Box 4/5/1, Angus Library, University of Oxford.

of wicked aversion to him. Their very mind and conscience are defiled. Their ideas of excellence and good and of the evil of sin are, as it were, obliterated.

I conceive that the whole Arminian, Socinian, and Antinomian systems, so far as I understand them, rest upon the supposition of these principles being false. So that if it should be found at last that God is an infinitely excellent being, worthy of being loved with all that love that his law requires; that as such, his law is entirely fair and equitable, and that for God to have required less would have been denying himself to be what he is; and if it should appear at last that man is utterly lost, and lies absolutely at the discretion of God; then the whole of these systems I think it is easy to prove must fall to the ground. . . . If the law of God is right and good, and arises from the very nature of God, Antinomianism cannot stand. And if we are such great sinners, we need a great Saviour, infinitely greater than the Socinian Saviour![33]

For Fuller, moral corruption of the will and false beliefs of the mind went hand in hand. Alternatively, a right knowledge and love of God and the embrace of the gospel provided the key to true virtue. Inevitably, therefore, Fuller took issue with the Enlightenment assault on the morality of traditional Christian beliefs.

"In Nature We See No Bounds to Our Inquiries": Fuller's Eighteenth-Century Enlightenment Moral Context

For many Enlightenment figures, the rejection of Christianity was a deeply moral matter.[34] Aside from repudiating its supernaturalism, many thinkers found Christianity dehumanizing. The eighteenth-century Enlightenment was largely preoccupied with finding a universal, egalitarian belief system—and according to this criteria, orthodox Christianity was inherently nonviable. The Christian God was unfair and discriminatory to require universal obedience while limiting access to his special divine revelation. Andrew Fuller, however, had labored to demonstrate in *The Gospel Worthy of All Acceptation* that Christianity's beliefs were in fact equitable and that they applied universally. Although he originally designed the work as a corrective to false thinking about moral accountability in

---

33. Quoted in Ryland, *Life and Death of the Rev. Andrew Fuller*, 40.

34. The quote in the subheading is from Priestley, *Importance and Extent of Free Inquiry*, 7.

The Love of God Holds Creation Together

Christian circles, its impact on his thought prepared him to defend the moral goodness of Christian doctrine in his late eighteenth-century British Enlightenment context.

Fuller wrote against two of the most widely known eighteenth-century critics of orthodox Christianity: Joseph Priestley and Thomas Paine. Although Priestley was a Socinian and Paine a Deist, they had a shared agenda to restore pure religion by replacing traditional Christian beliefs about God and human nature with more optimistic and enlightened ones. These men found Christian doctrine—especially Calvinism—a barrier to moral and social progress. The god of the Enlightenment was not the God of orthodox Christian belief.

According to Henry May, the various stages of the Enlightenment share two beliefs: that "the present age is more enlightened than the past," and that "we understand nature and man best through the use of our natural faculties."[35] May identifies the first stage as the Moderate Enlightenment, in which men like Isaac Newton (1642–1727) and Cotton Mather (1663–1728) alike could reconcile advances in science and confidence in human reason with orthodox Christianity. The second stage was the Skeptical Enlightenment of Britain and France, and its champions were David Hume (1711–1776) and François-Marie Arouet, a.k.a. Voltaire (1694–1778). They employed reason as a weapon to voice their sophisticated vitriol against traditional religion, but their influence was largely limited to the elitist class of the intelligentsia. May includes Priestley and Paine among the leaders of the third stage, the Revolutionary Enlightenment. These men built off the ideas of the Skeptical Enlightenment, and like Prometheus they brought the fire to the people. "Paine, unlike Toland or Tindal, Voltaire or Diderot, got his message to the masses."[36] Likewise, upon his conversion to Socinianism, Priestley wrote voluminous theological works "with no other view" than to "make proselytes."[37]

The Enlightenment repudiation of orthodox Christian belief created a vacuum for moral authority, necessitating the invocation of other rules and motives for virtuous living. This undertaking assumed various forms in British thought. For John Locke (1632–1704), humans apprehended morality by reason and through mathematical demonstration. The Earl of Shaftesbury argued that one detected goodness through an inherent moral

---

35. May, *Enlightenment in America*, xiv.
36. Ibid., 176.
37. Priestley, *Defences of Unitarianism*, 18:372.

sense; personal satisfaction and social harmony with fellow creatures was achievable by following one's natural inclination to benevolence. David Hume responded that reason itself could never motivate one to virtue. Rather, the innate human passions—such as sympathy, feeling, and desire—provided the spring for morality.[38] Thus, during this period, "'morality' became the name for that particular sphere in which rules of conduct which are neither theological nor legal nor aesthetic are allowed a cultural space of their own."[39] According to Alisdair MacIntyre, the "distinguishing of the moral from the theological" was a product of the Enlightenment project to assert an "independent rational justification of morality."[40] It would be misleadingly reductionist to say that Priestley and Paine—like all of these Enlightenment thinkers—conformed to a neatly categorized pattern of ethical thought. Even so, they clearly inherited the general modernist shift to replace the authority of revealed divine moral law with human nature as normative for morality.

The views of human nature in the eighteenth century heavily determined its ethical paradigms. Many Enlightenment thinkers "move from premises concerning human nature as they understand it to be to conclusions about the authority of moral rules and precepts."[41] They accepted an optimistic anthropology that conflicted with negative Christian notions of human inability—whether natural or moral. "Whereas Enlightenment

---

38. MacIntyre, *Short History of Ethics*, esp. 157–77. For more on eighteenth-century British ethical thought, see McNaughton, "British Moralists," 203–25.

39. MacIntyre, *After Virtue*, 39.

40. Ibid. MacIntyre goes on to argue, "The project of providing a rational vindication of morality had decisively failed; and from henceforward the morality of our predecessor culture—and subsequently of our own—lacked any public, shared rationale or justification. In a world of secular rationality religion could no longer provide such a shared background and foundation for moral discourse and action; and the failure of philosophy to provide what religion could no longer furnish was an important cause of philosophy losing its central cultural role and becoming a marginal, narrowly academic discipline" (ibid., 50). Whether or not one agrees with MacIntyre's assessment, his point that the Enlightenment largely inherited the same basic moral norms as the Protestantism it rejected is a helpful observation for the present study. Like Hume, Paine perpetuated many of the same Protestant ethical rules but he shifted their foundation from Christianity to the self and natural laws.

41. Ibid., 52. From this point MacIntyre states, "I want to argue that any project of this form was bound to fail, because of an ineradicable discrepancy between their shared conception of moral rules and precepts on the one hand and what was shared . . . in their conception of human nature on the other" (ibid.). Fuller shares this critique that their ethical project would fail largely because it rested on erroneous views of human nature.

thinkers enthusiastically sought knowledge and gloried in the achievements and capacities of man," Christian morality, notes Peter Jimack, "was based on the original sin of tasting of the fruit of the tree of knowledge, condemned the sin of pride and appeared to deplore most of man's natural inclinations."[42] The gap between Christian orthodoxy and the "new moral philosophy" was pronounced and irreconcilable.[43]

Priestley and Paine sympathized with the Enlightenment confidence in human capacity, and yet neither jettisoned religious belief. They considered both Christian orthodoxy and atheism irrational polar extremes; each system proved harmful and demeaning to human dignity and moral progress. These thinkers represented two strands of Enlightenment religion—Priestley of Rational Dissent and Paine of Deism—that attempted to uphold the new moral philosophy and redeem rational faith. Priestley and Paine had distinctive beliefs, political views, and agendas—but they found commonality in gaining reputations for their aggressive assaults on the immorality of traditional Christian belief.

Joseph Priestley and Rational Dissent

Joseph Priestley eludes simple analysis. John Brooke touches on Priestley's complexity in one long and accurate sentence:

> What is one to make of a man who proclaimed himself a Christian and denied the divinity of Christ; an apologist who considered this the best of all possible worlds and yet one which could be improved; a theist who denied that God could act directly on the human mind and yet who insisted that his God was more in control of human affairs than the God of religious orthodoxy; a Scriptural exegete who accepted the reality of certain biblical miracles as part of an argument to show that miracles did not occur; a philosophical determinist who believed that a denial of the autonomy of the human will made human beings more, not less, responsible for their actions; . . . a materialist who did not believe in matter . . . ; an empiricist . . . ; and overriding all, a radical in politics and religion,

---

42. Jimack, "French Enlightenment II," 251–73.

43. As Marsden succinctly explains, "The new moral philosophy was part of the modern project that made nature normative for understanding the self and self-understanding normative for morality." Marsden, *Jonathan Edwards*, 464–65.

and yet so conservative in his chemical theory that he was left picking nits in the new French system?[44]

Priestley's fascinating career and thought has drawn numerous studies,[45] but for the purposes of this study a brief introduction to his life will suffice since the point is to address his censure of Christian morality.

Priestley was born on March 13, 1733, in Yorkshire to Jonas, a clothworker, and Mary. After his mother died when he was seven years old, his aunt—who along with most of his family was a devoted Calvinist and a member of the Heckmondwike Congregational church—took responsibility for raising him. Although his aunt was a Calvinist, she encouraged Priestley to think for himself—a suggestion that he took seriously. By his teens, Priestley identified as an Arminian and subsequently as an Arian.[46] Priestley's developments in religious belief were largely based on his shifting anthropological views. The elders at the Heckmondwike church "refused me," Priestley recalled, "because when they interrogated me on the subject of the sin of Adam, I appeared not to be quite orthodox."[47] Priestley's confidence in human progress had little room for Calvinist notions of human inability.

In 1752, he entered the Daventry Academy, a Dissenting school for Non-Conformists who did not pass the religious test of Oxford or Cambridge.[48] While at Daventry, Priestley settled on many of his religious convictions. Consistent with the tradition of Rational Dissent, he simultaneously affirmed the authority of Scripture in "matters of faith" as well as the necessity for "rational and liberal sentiments" of God.[49] His motto was to question everything—he questioned his faith with science and his science with faith. He argued that the Bible was filled with historical errors and human corruptions, the Trinity was a logical contradiction—"since

---

44. Brooke, "'Sower Went Forth,'" 21–56.

45. For more on Priestley, see Schofield, *Enlightenment of Joseph Priestley*; Gibbs, *Joseph Priestley*; Bowers, *Priestley and English Unitarianism in America*; Tapper, "Priestley on Politics," 272–86; Hiebert, "Integration of Revealed Religion," 27–61; Brooke, "Joining Natural Philosophy to Christianity," 319–36; and McEvoy and McGuire, "God and Nature," 325–404. Also see Priestley, *Memoirs*, as well as Priestley, *Theological and Miscellaneous Works*.

46. Bowers, *Priestley and English Unitarianism in America*, 31.

47. Priestley, *Memoirs*, 7.

48. Schofield, *Enlightenment of Joseph Priestley*, 31–62.

49. Quoted in Bowers, *Priestley and English Unitarianism in America*, 31.

three cannot be one, or one, three"[50]—and the idea of the atonement was "a great dishonour to God" and an aberration from "his essential goodness."[51] Denying the deity of Christ, Priestley accused orthodox Christians of arrant idolatry for worshipping and praying to him.[52] Upon leaving Daventry, Priestley pursued his scientific and ministerial career, preaching to various congregations that God's "intention was that all should be happy."[53] His evolving views on the Trinity, the atonement, and anthropology led to his last conversion—from Arianism to Socinianism—in the 1760s while living in Leeds.[54]

Although Priestley is most known for his original contributions in science (he not only discovered oxygen but also ammonia and sulphur dioxide, and he invented soda-water),[55] he placed a higher value on "the identity and purification of Christianity than on the identity and purification of gases."[56] In his lifetime, Priestley ministered to five dissenting congregations, filled volumes with his theological thought, and he largely furnished the Unitarian movement with its liturgical and devotional literature. While Priestley was at a dinner party in Paris, a writer pointed to some rogue bishops and said, "they are no more believers than you or I."[57] Priestley snapped back insisting that he was in fact a Christian, showing that even his contemporaries had difficulty categorizing him.

The theme of progress permeated Priestley's thought, and his ethics were no exception. As Brooke notes, Priestley believed that "scientific progress was not merely a model but a vehicle for social and religious reform."[58] Priestley wrote, "In nature we see no bounds to our inquiries. One discovery always hints of many more, and brings us into a wider field of speculation. Now why should this not be . . . the case with respect to knowledge of a moral and religious kind?"[59] The individual must employ rigorous research to discover religious and moral truth and discipline to implement it.

50. Priestley, *Defences of Unitarianism*, 19:108.
51. Quoted in Watts, *Dissenters*, 474.
52. See Haykin, "Socinian and a Calvinist Compared," 178–98.
53. Brooke, "Joining Natural Philosophy to Christianity," 323.
54. Bowers, *Joseph Priestley*, 32.
55. Watts, *Dissenters*, 472.
56. Brooke, "Joining Natural Philosophy to Christianity," 323.
57. Quoted in May, *Enlightenment in America*, 158.
58. Brooke, "Joining Natural Philosophy to Christianity," 320.
59. Priestley, *Importance and Extent of Free Inquiry*, 7.

Although Priestley's theodicy acknowledged the reality of evil in creation, his millenarianism—which stressed future hope through human progress—ultimately prevailed. He proposed that the "human virtues can only be acquired in a struggle against adversity," and since "history shows divine providence steadily bringing good out of evil" in a constant "process of amelioration," humanity can confidently aspire to future moral triumph.[60] Priestley urged the individual self to mature his or her virtue in a struggle with evil, and one of the main tools for this end was education, "that of enlightening the minds of men."[61] Priestley represented "a change of disposition and character as being effected only by a change of conduct, and that of long continuance."[62] Through education and self-discipline, humanity had the resources and the natural capacity for moral excellence and happiness.

His confidence in human nature to progress in virtue clashed with the Calvinist teaching that the unregenerate lacked the ability to perform God's will. According to the "doctrine of reason," Priestley maintained, "nothing is requisite to make men, in all situations, the objects of [God's] favor, but such moral conduct as he has made them capable of."[63] Since Priestley's "gospel was concerned with the reformation of character," he allowed no category in "his rational system for any doctrine that promised sudden acceptance of God."[64] Priestley taught that humans had the inherent capacity for improvement in not only politics and science but also in religion and morality.

For Priestley, Calvinist beliefs undermined human potential for progress in morality.

> Admitting the truth of a Trinity of persons in the Godhead, original sin, arbitrary predestination, atonement by the death of Christ, and the plenary inspiration of the Scriptures; their value, estimated by their influence on the morals of men, cannot be supposed, even by the admirers of them, to be of any moment, compared to the doctrine of the resurrection of the human race to a life of retribution: and, in the opinion of those who reject them, they have a very unfavourable tendency; giving wrong impressions concerning the character and moral government of

---

60. Tapper, "Priestley on Politics, Progress and Moral Theology," 274.
61. Priestley, *Proper Objects of Education*, 438–39.
62. Quoted in Fuller, *Calvinistic and Socinian Systems Examined*, in *WAF*, 2:145.
63. Priestley, *History of the Corruptions of Christianity*, 154–55.
64. Brooke, "Joining Natural Philosophy to Christianity," 326.

> God, and such as might tend, if they have any effect, to relax the obligations of virtue.[65]

Therefore, he advocated Socinianism as a positive alternative to Calvinism in order to motivate social and moral advancement.

> It is certainly a great satisfaction to entertain such an idea of the author of the universe, and of his moral government, as is consonant to the dictates of reason and the tenor of revelation in general.... This is a simple and pleasing view of God and his moral government, and the consideration of it cannot but have the best effect on the temper of our minds and conduct in life.[66]

In light of Calvinism's repelling notions of God and its debilitating views of human ability, "I do not see," Priestley expressed, "what motive a Calvinist can have to give any attention to his moral conduct.... If any system of speculative principles can operate as an axe at the root of all virtue and goodness, it is this."[67] For Priestley, Christ's person and atonement had little to do with human morality, "The recovery of genuine Christianity from this deplorably corrupted state to the rational views we now entertain of it ... cannot but impress the thoughtful and pious minds with sentiments of wonder."[68] The incentive for virtue rested in rational doctrine, not polluted Calvinist dogma.

Thomas Paine and Deism

Thomas Paine did not have the originality and scientific genius of Joseph Priestley. Rather, Paine's contribution lay in his gift to recast Enlightenment ideology into a revolutionary, utopian vision for broader audiences.[69] Like Fuller and Priestley, Paine emerged from his humble background to a

---

65. Quoted in Fuller, *Calvinistic and Socinian Systems Examined*, in *WAF*, 2:112–13.
66. Priestley, *History of the Corruptions of Christianity*, 154–55.
67. Quoted in Fuller, *Calvinistic and Socinian Systems Examined*, in *WAF*, 2:142.
68. Priestley, *General History of the Christian Church*, 10:532.
69. For biographies on Paine, see Fruchtman, *Apostle of Freedom*; Powell, *Greatest Exile*; Keane, *Tom Paine*; and for an old but classic work, see Conway, *Life of Thomas Paine*. On the intellectual context of the Revolutionary era and Deism, see Wills, *Inventing America*; White, *Philosophy of the American Revolution*; and Walters, *American Deists*. On Paine's thought, see Claeys, *Thomas Paine*; Foner, *Paine and Revolutionary America*; Aldridge, *Paine's American Ideology*; and Kuklick, *Thomas Paine*. On his religious ideology, see Hoselton, "Thomas Paine and Democratic Religion," 11–26.

position of considerable influence. Born at Thetford, England in 1737 to a family of Quakers, Paine followed his father's occupation as a corset maker at a young age. In the first four decades of his life, he worked as a common sailor, a schoolteacher, operated a small tobacco shop, and served as an excise officer for the English government. In 1774, after his second marriage had failed, he moved to America. Before he left England, he fortuitously met Benjamin Franklin in London, from whom he obtained a recommendation letter that earned him immediate employment in America as a printer and editor in Pennsylvania. Shortly after his arrival, Paine joined the cause for independence, and his position as an editor afforded him the opportunity to voice his protest.

In January 1776, Paine published the well-known political pamphlet, *Common Sense*.[70] In this work, Paine drew from an Enlightenment understanding of human nature and channeled it into "a new rhetoric of radical egalitarianism."[71] A century earlier, John Locke argued that there was "nothing more evident, than that creatures of the same species and rank promiscuously born to all the same advantages of nature, and the use of the same faculties, should also be equal one amongst another without subordination or subjection."[72] Paine perceived and articulated dramatic social implications from this Enlightenment anthropology, and thus he was determined to persuade the colonist masses that they shared the same humanity—and therefore the same natural rights—as royalty.[73]

Paine sowed his religious revolution in the same soil as his political revolution: the equality of humankind.[74] In Part I of *The Age of Reason*, written in 1793, Paine recalled how after writing *Common Sense* he had anticipated that "a revolution in the system of government would be followed by a revolution in the system of religion."[75] He wrote *The Age of Reason* in

---

70. Paine's *Common Sense* had a massive impact on the American political conscience. It was the best-selling pamphlet of the Revolutionary period. Calkin, "Pamphlets and Public Opinion," 38–40. John Adams commented that *Common Sense* "was received in France and in all Europe with Rapture." From the entry dated February 11, 1779, in Adams, *Diary and Autobiography of John Adams*, 2:351.

71. Thompson, *Making of the English Working Class*, 103, 121.

72. Locke, *Second Treatise*, chap. II, sect. 4., quoted in White, *Philosophy of the American Revolution*, 66.

73. Fruchtman, "Nature and Revolution," 421–38.

74. Ian Harris rightly identifies "two revolutions" in Paine's thinking, "one in religion to complement the one in government." Harris, "Paine and Burke," 51.

75. Paine, *Age of Reason*, 269. Paine published *The Age of Reason* in two parts: Part I

order to stir this religious revolution and steer it away from both atheism and Christianity, "lest, in the general wreck of superstition, of false systems of government, and false theology, we lose sight of morality, of humanity, and of the theology that is true."[76] For Paine, the "theology that is true" consisted of a very concise creed: "I believe in one God and no more; and I hope for happiness beyond this life. I believe in the equality of man, and I believe that religious duties consist in doing justice, loving mercy, and endeavoring to make our fellow-creatures happy."[77] As for his ecclesiology, he declared, "My own mind is my own church."[78] He then proceeded for the rest of the work to list and deride the things he did not believe.

Paine's rejection of revelation serves as a lens for understanding his religious views and his critique that Christian doctrine was inherently immoral. Ian Harris offers a helpful assessment of Paine's repudiation of revelation.

> Paine thought revelation false. He conceived that nature provided the same pattern of benefits for all. The truths which man could discover through his natural faculties were in principle transparent to everyone and those truths were sufficient for all serious purposes. Distinctions between persons were not authorised by nature, which intended everyone to have the same standing. Accordingly, the artificial differences which ecclesiastical, political, and social artifice had created bespoke the history of imposture and oppression. By contrast reference to the original and natural organization of mankind would disclose the antidote to such modern perversions. That antidote was republicanism and free religion: the former reflected man's natural equality, and the latter left him free to exercise his natural faculties in choosing his religion. Hence, disposing of the past was the condition of improvement.[79]

Paine, like most Deists, took it for granted that in order for God to be good, his revelation cannot be partial. As Charles Blount (1654–1693), a seventeenth-century Deist, expressed, "That Rule which is necessary to our

---

in 1794, and Part II in 1795. As Paine wrote Part I, he did not have access to a Bible. Thus, he wrote Part II to extend his criticisms on the Old and New Testament texts once he obtained one. This study focuses on Part I because it pertains more directly to his religious and moral views.

76. Ibid., 267.
77. Ibid.
78. Ibid., 268.
79. Harris, "Paine and Burke," 51.

future Happiness, ought to be generally made known to all men. Therefore no Revealed Religion is necessary to future Happiness."[80] Likewise, the Deist Matthew Tindal (1657–1733) wrote, "Can God, who equally beholds all the Dwellers on Earth, free from any partiality and prejudice, make some People his favourites" by giving them unique revelation of the truth "while others, far the greater number, shall . . . want this favour?"[81] Paine and other Deists judged revelation intrinsically immoral because it discriminated between equal beings; hence his aggressive labors to disprove the verity of Scripture in *The Age of Reason*.

Paine's goal was to democratize truth by reducing religious knowledge to universal facts. For Paine, "A thing which everybody is required to believe requires that the proof and evidence of it should be equal to all, and universal."[82] Unlike revelation, all humanity had equal access to reason and to creation. By employing natural reason to contemplate creation, everyone could ascertain "that God is a God of truth and justice,"[83] and that the "only idea we can have of serving God is that of contributing to the happiness of the living creation that God has made."[84] These principles constituted unadulterated religion. Paine denied the Trinity because it did not meet his egalitarian criteria—while peoples worldwide varied in the number of gods they affirmed, everyone could employ their natural faculties and recognize a single deity.[85] Paine also denied the necessity of redemption on the basis of his egalitarianism. "Moral justice cannot take the innocent for the guilty, even if the innocent would offer itself," and everyone "stands in the same relative condition with his Maker . . . since man existed."[86] Paine repudiated the truth of Christian doctrine because it contradicted his moral axioms and his optimistic anthropology.

Paine rested the standard of morality on an impartial, benevolent God. "The practice of moral truth, or in other words a practical imitation of the moral goodness of God, is no other than our acting towards each other as he

---

80. Quoted in Harris, "Paine and Burke," 38.

81. Tindal, *Christianity as Old as Creation* (1730), quoted in Harris, "Paine and Burke," 39.

82. Paine, *Age of Reason*, 272.

83. Paine, "Examination of Prophecies," 357.

84. Paine, *Age of Reason*, 311.

85. Ibid., 294.

86. Ibid., 285.

acts benignly towards all."[87] Man's moral duty consisted of "imitating [God] in everything moral, scientific, and mechanical."[88] Paine found his moral exemplar in none other than the impartial Jesus of Nazareth. "Jesus Christ founded no new system. He called men to the practice of moral virtues, and the belief of one God. The great trait in his character is philanthropy."[89] Paine rested enormous confidence in human nature to embrace the truth and lead moral lives as long as man had freedom. He thus devoted his life to overthrowing oppressive political and religious authorities in order to liberate humanity to fulfill its social and moral potential. Humans possessed the natural resources for moral excellence and happiness, but Christianity's inequitable doctrines suppressed this potential.

Conclusion

In *The Gospel Worthy of All Acceptation*, Fuller agreed that humanity possessed the natural ability to ascertain religious and moral truth. However, when it came to human moral ability to embrace true virtue, his stance could not have been more at odds with radical Enlightenment figures like Priestley and Paine. The opposing positions fundamentally clashed on anthropology. In Priestley and Paine's estimation of human nature, the individual self possessed a remarkable capacity for moral progress. On the other hand, Fuller's anthropology stressed the will's corrupt moral inclination, necessitating the very Evangelical Calvinist doctrines that Priestley and Paine rendered immoral. The contrasting anthropologies also determined very different missions for these figures. For Priestley and Paine, their mission was to tear down traditional authoritarian structures and instruct the masses in realizing their inherent social and moral potential. Meanwhile Fuller, convinced that the knowledge and love of God alone possessed the power to transform hearts and lives, committed his life to advancing the spread of the gospel in the world.

---

87. Ibid., 311.
88. Ibid., 302.
89. Ibid., 282.

3

"Religion that Inspires the Love of God": Fuller's Aretegenic Orthodoxy

IN THE FORMATIVE STAGES of his early ministry, Andrew Fuller determined that humanity was morally accountable to the Creator for its rebellion.[1] Human beings cannot obey God's righteous law because man's evil inclinations frustrate any sincere decision for moral good. In contrast to Enlightenment thinkers like Joseph Priestley and Thomas Paine, the ethical issue for Fuller was not that people were heeding orthodox Christianity but rejecting it. The optimistic and rational Enlightenment understanding of human nature had no moral necessity for special divine revelation or spiritual redemption. In Fuller's anthropology, however, Evangelical truth served as a *sine qua non* of true virtue—humanity desperately needed God to be good. This chapter explores Fuller's response to Priestley and Paine and how his understanding of the relationship between Christian doctrine and virtue grounded his theology of virtue.

"Christ Is of More Than Ordinary Importance": Fuller on Socinianism

In 1791, Fuller reflected in a diary entry, "I have lately been employed in reading several Socinian writers, Lindsey, Priestly [sic], Belsham, &c. and have employed myself in penning down thoughts on the moral tendency of their system."[2] Many late eighteenth-century ministers, especially in the

---

1. The quote in the chapter title is from Fuller, *Gospel Its Own Witness*, in WAF, 2:7.
2. Ryland, *Life and Death of the Rev. Andrew Fuller*, 214. The quote in the subheading

Dissenting tradition, digested the Socinian writings. Two Particular Baptist ministers, Robert Robinson (1735–1790) and James Lyons (1768–1824), surprised the church community when they deserted orthodoxy, resigned their pastorates, and joined the Socinian cause.[3] Robinson, a former convert of George Whitefield (1714–1770) and pastor of the historic St. Andrew's Street Baptist Church in Cambridge, preached his final sermons deriding trinitarianism at Socinian meeting houses. According to Priestley, Robinson's tirade "savoured rather of the burlesque, than serious reasoning."[4] Fuller's study of the Socinians produced the opposite effect, "I found an increasing aversion to their views of things, and I feel the ground on which my hopes are built more solid than ever."[5]

Christology was such a heated subject matter in the late eighteenth century that "books were put into" Fuller's hands the first year of his ministry concerning Christ's pre-existence, the virgin birth, Christ's human soul, and his Sonship.[6] From his reading Fuller concluded two points—Christ was pre-existent in his divine nature and not in the form of a human soul like the Arians taught, and Christ as the Son of God was equal with the Father in all the divine attributes. These Christological principles implied that "everything pertaining to the person of Christ is of more than ordinary importance."[7] Fuller's learning in Christology pervaded every area of his theology. He later remarked that if he had "not been initiated into these principles at an early period, I should not have been able to write the treatise against Socinianism."[8]

In 1793, Fuller published *The Calvinistic and Socinian Systems Examined and Compared, As to Their Moral Tendency, In a Series of Letters, Addressed to the Friends of Vital and Practical Religion.*[9] In his introductory

---

is from ibid., 52.

3. For more on the conversions of Robinson and Lyons to Socinianism, see Haykin, "Socinian and a Calvinist Compared," 178–98.

4. Quoted in Oliver, "Emergence of a Strict and Particular Baptist Community," 71 n. 143.

5. Quoted in Ryland, *Life and Death of the Rev. Andrew Fuller*, 214.

6. Ibid., 52.

7. Ibid.

8. Ibid., 54.

9. Fuller, *Calvinistic and Socinian Systems Examined*, in WAF, 2:108–242. The WAF republished the 2nd ed. from 1802, which I will use. The 2nd ed. is mainly the same in substance as the first. Fuller writes, "The author has attempted, in some places, to strengthen his argument, and to remove such objections as have hitherto occurred,"

remarks, Fuller acknowledged the amount of ink that had already been spilt on the Socinian controversy, "the Christian world, to a considerable degree, has been drawn towards it."[10] Nonetheless, determined that "the prevalence of truth is a good that will outweigh all the ills that may have attended its discovery," Fuller found it necessary to add his voice to the debate.[11] As a polemicist, Fuller had little tolerance for a latitudinarian spirit. When charged with bigotry for his unwavering convictions, Fuller responded that promoting the truth conveyed more love than efforts at groundless unity. "One thing in particular I would pray for," Fuller meditated in his diary, "that I may not only be kept from erroneous principles, but may so love the truth as never to keep it back."[12]

Fuller had no interest in merely recycling the arguments of others. In search of an innovative contribution, he approached the debate on the level of how the principles of each system impacted "the heart and life" of its followers.[13] Fuller accepted Priestley's axiom that "the value or importance of religious principles is to be estimated by their influence on the morals of men."[14] Having read enough about the immorality of Calvinist doctrine, Fuller flipped the debate on its head, "By this rule let the forementioned doctrines, with their opposites, be tried."[15] Fuller accepted Priestley's moral test of true doctrine, but he drew very different conclusions.

While Fuller treated several of the Calvinist doctrines under interrogation, his central argument rested on the person and work of Christ.

> Take away Christ; nay, take away the deity and atonement of Christ; and the whole ceremonial of the Old Testament appears to us little more than a dead mass of uninteresting matter: prophecy loses all that is interesting and endearing: the gospel is annihilated, or ceases to be that good news to lost sinners which it professes to be; practical religion is divested of its most powerful motives; the evangelical dispensation of its peculiar glory; and heaven itself of its most transporting joys.[16]

---

especially in Letters IV and XV. Ibid., 2:111. Fuller added a new preface and he responded to Joshua Toulmin, John Kentish, and Thomas Belsham's critical reviews in a postscript.

10. Ibid., 2:112.

11. Ibid.

12. Quoted in Ryland, *Life and Death of the Rev. Andrew Fuller*, 204.

13. Fuller, *Calvinistic and Socinian Systems Examined*, in WAF, 2:112.

14. Quoted in ibid., 2:112–13.

15. Ibid., 2:112.

16. Ibid., 2:191–92.

The Love of God Holds Creation Together

By abandoning belief in the deity and atonement of Christ, Socinianism robbed Christianity of its lifeblood. For Fuller, Christ's deity grounded the efficacy of his atoning work to save sinners and transform them to reflect the good character of God. Socinians replaced Christ as Savior for unrighteous humanity with Christ as moral exemplar for a progressing humanity.

While Fuller received a degree of resistance from the Christian community for *The Gospel Worthy of All Acceptation*, his tract against Socinianism met with such an "unusual tide of respect and applause" that Fuller remembered having to "watch his own heart" for pride.[17] Although many have considered the work "the most celebrated of Fuller's writings," he did not obtain the same flattery from the Socinians.[18] Ryland explained the reaction, "the Socinians, who had so frequently indulged themselves in inveighing, with the utmost vehemence, against the licentious tendency of the Calvinistic system, were much disturbed at having the charge turned against themselves. It was now considered as an unfair argument."[19] The Socinian thinker Thomas Belsham (1750–1829) assured Joseph Priestley that the treatise "was well worthy of his perusal," but Priestley never responded to it.[20] In July 1791, a three day-long riot erupted in Priestley's town of Birmingham. A group of Dissenters had campaigned to repeal the Test and Corporation Acts, a move that many English affiliated with the mischief of the French Revolution. The mobs razed the New Meeting House where Priestley ministered, subsequently moving on to his home where they destroyed his library and laboratory. Fuller condemned those who participated in the riot as "men of no principle" and not representative of true Christian conduct.[21] Priestley fled to London and then emigrated to America in 1794, shortly after Fuller published his work.[22] Perhaps Priestley's departure accounts for his silence; for he, like Fuller, was not one to shrink from a good debate.

Other prominent Socinian leaders eventually broke the silence. In 1796 Joshua Toulmin (1740–1815)[23] published *The Practical Efficacy of the Unitarian Doctrine Considered, in a Series of Letters to the Rev. Andrew*

---

17. Quoted in Ryland, *Life and Death of the Rev. Andrew Fuller*, 214–15.
18. Everts, "Andrew Fuller," 416.
19. Ryland, *Life and Death of the Rev. Andrew Fuller*, 215–16.
20. Quoted in Fuller, *Reflections on Mr. Belsham's Review*, in *WAF*, 2:288.
21. Fuller, *Calvinistic and Socinian Systems Examined*, in *WAF*, 2:111.
22. Watts, *Dissenters*, 1:486–87.
23. For more on Toulmin, see Wykes, "Joshua Toulmin," 224–43.

Fuller.²⁴ Toulmin attended the Calvinist-supported Hoxton Dissenting Academy, where he challenged the school's beliefs even as a student.²⁵ He published many historical works, and he ministered at the New Meeting House in Birmingham along with John Kentish in the early 1800s. In his response to Fuller, Toulmin insisted on the label Unitarian rather than Socinian since they derived their views not from Faustus Socinus but from primitive Christianity. He proceeded to argue that unlike later fabricated Calvinist principles—like human depravity, the atonement, and the deity of Christ—Unitarian doctrine originated from the apostolic tradition. After listing men of genuine piety who did not adhere to Calvinism, Toulmin concluded, "the Calvinist system is not essential for devotion."²⁶

In July 1796 John Kentish (1768–1853) delivered *The Moral Tendency of the Genuine Christian Doctrine* before the West of England Society of Unitarian Christians at Bow Meeting-house in Exeter.²⁷ Kentish was educated under the Socinian Thomas Belsham at both the Daventry Dissenting Academy and Hackney College. He assumed various ministry positions until he accepted a call to the New Meeting House in Birmingham along with Toulmin.²⁸ Kentish stressed that belief in Unitarian views on the nature of God and Jesus Christ instilled superior holiness and morality. Although Unitarians may express their admiration differently, they esteem "the goodness of the Almighty exhibited in the works of nature, in the dispensations of providence, and in our temporal comfort" just as much as any other "class of Christians."²⁹ Unlike orthodox Christians who confused love and conformity to Christ with love for God, the Unitarians' devotion to the one true God provided "a powerful motive to the most willing obedience."³⁰ *Contra* Fuller, Unitarianism reflected the apostolic tradition more than Calvinism and it inclined towards true piety.

In 1797 Fuller published his reply to Toulmin and Kentish in *Socinianism Indefensible on the Ground of its Moral Tendency*.³¹ Fuller accused Toulmin of shifting the ground of argument by not directly addressing the

---

24. Toulmin, *Practical Efficacy of the Unitarian Doctrine*.
25. Sell, "Andrew Fuller and the Socinians," 126–28.
26. Toulmin, *Practical Efficacy of the Unitarian Doctrine*, 71.
27. Kentish, *Moral Tendency of Christian Doctrine*, 6.
28. Sell, "Andrew Fuller and the Socinians," 128–30.
29. Kentish, *Moral Tendency of Christian Doctrine*, 12.
30. Ibid., 13.
31. Fuller, *Socinianism Indefensible*, in *WAF*, 2:243–287.

points he raised in *Calvinistic and Socinian Systems Examined*. Toulmin focused on citing scriptural supports for Socinian doctrine, a tactic that Fuller deemed irrelevant to the discussion at hand since most Socinians believed that the Bible "was never designed to decide upon controverted questions in religion and morality."[32] He then proceeded to defend his reasons for grounding the debate in moral reasoning.[33] Fuller applauded Kentish for engaging his arguments on the established grounds; however, he found his review lacking in robustness, deeming it "a retreat . . . rather than a pitched battle."[34] At the heart of his reply to Kentish, Fuller countered that one could not truly love God without a proper knowledge and esteem of Jesus Christ's deity and atonement. Christians love God "on account of the infinite amiableness of his moral character, as displayed particularly in the gospel, or (as the Scripture express it) of 'the glory of God in the face of Jesus Christ.'"[35] In order to grow in virtue, one must study the expression of God's moral character in the person and work of Jesus Christ.

Shortly after Fuller responded to Toulmin and Kentish, he wrote a brief essay entitled *The Deity of Christ Essential to Atonement*.[36] Although the essay was not a direct reply to a particular Socinian work, it succinctly addressed why the deity of Christ was crucial to the debate. For Fuller, "the Deity and atonement of Christ have always . . . stood or fallen together;" and when they sank, "every other important doctrine of the gospel" followed.[37] He considered the deity and atonement of Christ "fundamental truths" that grounded vital Christian belief and practice.[38] While wicked humanity "is totally incompetent to answer the character of a saviour," Christ's sinless divine and human natures qualified him to satisfy God's "Divine justice" against human rebellion through his atoning death.[39] Without the deity of Christ, sinful humans had no hope of true reconciliation with a good God and therefore no grounds for authentic knowledge and love of him.

---

32. Ibid., 2:244.

33. According to the verdict of Fuller's biographer, J. W. Morris, Toulmin "was scarcely a breakfast for his antagonist." Morris, *Memoirs of the Life and Death of the Rev. Andrew Fuller*, 262.

34. Fuller, *Socinianism Indefensible*, in WAF, 2:263.

35. Ibid., 2:273. Fuller cited 2 Cor 4:6.

36. Fuller, *Deity of Christ*, in WAF, 3:693–97.

37. Ibid., 3:695.

38. Ibid.

39. Ibid., 3:693, 697.

In 1798, Kentish wrote *Strictures Upon the Reply of Mr. A. Fuller to Mr. Kentish's Discourse, Entitled "The Moral Tendency of the Genuine Christian Doctrine."*[40] He reiterated many of his earlier points but with more force, emphasizing that he did not address the atonement because it did not play a central role in a discussion on morality. In a new appendix to his 1801 edition of *The Practical Efficacy of the Unitarian Doctrine*, Toulmin charged Fuller with sectarianism. Thomas Belsham dismissed Fuller's method as pharisaical in a critical review of William Wilberforce's (1759–1833)[41] *Treatise on Christianity*, to which Fuller briefly replied in *Reflections on Mr. Belsham's Review of Mr. Wilberforce's Treatise on Christianity*.[42] Fuller considered the charge a misrepresentation of his project, reminding Belsham that the Socinian leaders began the debate on the grounds of moral tendencies.[43] Fuller attempted to add the final word in a Postscript to the 1802 edition of *Calvinistic and Socinian Systems Examined and Compared*, in which he summed up his opponents' arguments, declared them unsatisfactory, and rehearsed his conviction that Calvinist doctrine was most conducive to moral excellence and happiness.[44]

"A Religion from God": Fuller on Deism and the Holy Nature of Scripture

In 1790 the British political philosopher Edmund Burke (1729–1797) inquired, "Who, born within the last forty years, has read one word of Collins, and Toland, and Tindal . . . and that whole race who called themselves Freethinkers? Who now reads Bolingbroke? Ask the booksellers of London what is become of all these lights of the world."[45] As Alan Sell notes, De-

---

40. Kentish, *Strictures*.

41. William Wilberforce, the eighteenth-century British Member of Parliament well known for his abolitionism and Evangelicalism, was a close acquaintance of Fuller. Wilberforce, who came from a considerably wealthier background than Fuller, described him as "the very picture of a blacksmith" and yet the "soundest and most creatively useful theologian" of the English Calvinistic Baptist tradition. Quoted Haykin, *One Heart and One Soul*, 152.

42. Fuller, *Reflections on Mr. Belsham's Review*, in WAF, 2:288–91.

43. Ibid., 2:288–90.

44. Fuller, *Calvinistic and Socinian Systems Examined*, in WAF, 2:234–42. For a more in-depth analysis on the exchanges between Fuller and the Socinians, see Sell, "Andrew Fuller and the Socinians," 119–34.

45. Burke, *Reflections on the Revolution in France*, 5:170–71. The quote in the

ism never gained much momentum as a religious movement or even as a defined school of thought in eighteenth-century Britain.[46] However, four years after Burke posed his challenge, Thomas Paine's first volume of *The Age of Reason* breathed new life into the controversy.[47]

John Ryland Jr. (1753–1825), one of Fuller's closest friends and a fellow minister in the Northamptonshire Baptist Association, had written Fuller the same year as *The Age of Reason* was published asking if he had read it. Fuller, who had suffered a minor paralytic stroke the year before,[48] responded,

> You ask, if I have seen Paine's *Age of Reason*. I have not. You do not know what reading is to me; one hour would bring on the headache. A newspaper is as much as I can read at a time. I could do many things, if strength would allow it. Plans of various works have entered my mind; but all must be dropped, or nearly so, for want of strength. Reading is worse to me, than thinking or writing.[49]

Although the stroke afflicted him with headaches throughout the rest of his life, he eventually digested Paine's work and replied to it in a sermon based on Heb 5:12–14 entitled *The Nature and Importance of an Intimate Knowledge of Divine Truth* (1796).[50] "Knowledge is every where [sic] encouraged in the Bible," Fuller asserted, "our best interests are interwoven with it; and the spirituality of our minds, and the real enjoyment of our lives, depend upon its increase."[51] His central argument maintained that the standard of truth and vital holiness resided in the infallible Scriptures that the Deists had rejected.

Fuller published a more extensive and systematic answer to Paine in *The Gospel Its Own Witness, or, The Holy Nature and Divine Harmony of the Christian Religion Contrasted with the Immorality and Absurdity of Deism*

---

subheading is from Fuller, *Gospel Its Own Witness*, in *WAF*, 2:7.

46. Sell, "Deism, Thomas Paine and Andrew Fuller," 111–43. Sell provides insightful historical background to Deist thought in seventeenth- and eighteenth-century Britain.

47. Prochaska listed at least thirty responses to Paine before 1800, but he failed to mention Fuller's contribution. Prochaska, "Thomas Paine's *The Age of Reason* Revisited," 561–76.

48. For a work on the background behind Fuller's polemic with Deism, see Haykin, "Oracles of God," 122–38.

49. Quoted in Ryland, *Life and Death of the Rev. Andrew Fuller*, 214–15.

50. Fuller, *Intimate Knowledge of Divine Truth*, in *WAF*, 1:160–74.

51. Ibid., 1:160.

(1799).[52] Although the treatise served as a response to *The Age of Reason*, Fuller aimed his conclusions at the overall Enlightenment vilification of Christian orthodoxy—lumping figures like "Shaftesbury, Tindal, Morgan, Bolingbroke, Voltaire, Hume, and Gibbon" into his critique.[53] He applied similar moral reasoning as his contest with the Socinians, but his arguments had gained more concision and cogency since he had first delivered them. Since the Deists were not like the Socinians in maintaining the Christian label while undermining its central doctrines, Fuller did not need to spend time debating the authenticity of his opponents' Christian identity or their devotion to the Scriptures.

Fuller divided his case into two parts. In the first part he contrasted the tendencies of Christianity and Deism to foster virtue, and in the second he defended the verity of Scripture on the basis of its internal consistency and its congruity with history and reason.

> If Christianity can be proved to be a religion that inspires the love of God and man; yea, and the only religion in the world that does so; if it endues the mind of him that embraces it with a principle of justice, meekness, chastity, and goodness, and even gives a tone to the morals of society at large; it will appear to carry its evidence along with it. The effects which it produces will be its letters of recommendation, written, "not with ink, but with the Spirit of the living God; not in tables of stone, but in the fleshly tables of the heart [2 Cor 3:3]." Moreover, if Christianity can be proved to be in harmony with itself, correspondent with observation and experience, and consistent with the clearest dictates of sober reason, it will further appear to carry in it its own evidence; come through whose hands it may, it will evince itself to be what it professes to be—a religion from God.[54]

The second part of this quote appears to be explicitly informed by Enlightenment rationalism and empiricism, as Fuller claimed to rest the truth of Christianity upon "observation and experience" as well as "the dictates of sober reason." However, while Fuller employed some of the language, the second part of *The Gospel Its Own Witness* bears very little resemblance to an Enlightenment empiricist approach. He maintained throughout the second part of the treatise that moral corruption polluted human reason and

---

52. Fuller, *Gospel Its Own Witness*, in WAF, 2:1–107.
53. Ibid., 2:5.
54. Ibid., 2:7.

its disposition, showing the necessity of the gospel to restore right thinking. He thus did very little to develop a neutral scientific or empiricist apology for Christianity. Rather, his main design was to defend Christianity against claims of being irrational and to present it as a coherent and compelling system. His final paragraph of the section showed clearly that Fuller was far from a strict Enlightenment empiricist or rationalist.

> Philosophy, at most, can only place us at the top of Pisgah: there, like Moses, we must die; it gives us no possession of the good land. It is the province of Christianity to add, "All is yours!" When you have ascended to the height of human discovery, there are things, and things of infinite moment too, that are utterly beyond its reach. Revelation is the medium, and the only medium, by which, standing as it were, "on nature's Alps," we discover things which eye hath not seen, nor ear heard, and of which it never hath entered into the heart of man to conceive.[55]

Fuller aimed to reclaim reason for Christian theology, defining it within a right understanding of God and human nature. For Fuller, the quest for truth was not reduced to a scientific exercise. He contrasted his method with Priestley, who believed that disinterested objectivity and detached rationalism offered the key to ascertaining truth and right doctrine. "An unbiased temper of mind is attained in consequence of becoming more indifferent to religion in general, and to all the modes and doctrines of it."[56] Fuller addressed *The Calvinistic and Socinian Systems Examined* to the "friends of vital and practical religion" out of a conviction that "true piety" enabled better judgment of true doctrine. Fuller wrote, "godly men are the only proper judges of Divine truth, being the only humble, upright, and earnest inquirers after it," quoting the words of Jesus in John 7:17 to support his claim, "it is 'he that doeth his will that shall know of his doctrine.'"[57] Fuller heavily emphasized the role that moral character played in determining belief, thus eliminating any notion of pure disinterested

---

55. Ibid., 2:97. In this way Fuller resembled Edwards's approach in *Original Sin*. As Norman Fiering observes, while Edwards claimed to prove the innate depravity of human nature "according to such rules and methods of reasoning, as are universally made use of . . . in experimental philosophy" and "reason from experience and facts," he ultimately never fully delivered on his promise and instead grounded his argument in non-empirical *a priori* theological notions of human nature and sin. See Fiering, *Jonathan Edwards's Moral Thought*, 49–61; and Edwards, *Original Sin*, 3:167.

56. Quoted in Fuller, *Calvinistic and Socinian Systems Examined*, in *WAF*, 2:108.

57. Ibid., 2:108.

rationalism. He believed that right reason must be tied with an interest in holiness and the love of God.

For Fuller, Christianity's intrinsic goodness and sensible logic bore witness to its veracity. Critics have condemned a phantom Christianity—"as it is corrupted by popish superstition, or as interwoven with national establishments"—but true and unadulterated Christianity was ultimately impregnable.[58] As Fuller declared to Paine, "Your directing your artillery chiefly against its corruptions and abuses, betray a consciousness that the thing itself, if not invulnerable, is yet not so easy of attack."[59] Fuller proceeded to defend authentic Christian belief and the reliability of Scripture on the basis of its divine origin and moral nature.

The Gospel Its Own Witness did not provoke the same reaction as his works against Socinianism. Like Priestley—coincidentally—Paine moved to America two years after Fuller published his apology, never offering a response. Unlike Priestley, Paine's friends did not rise to defend him. Even Fuller's early biographers had little to say about the work. After detailing Fuller's ministerial labors and his reaction to the events surrounding his son Robert's death, Andrew Gunton Fuller briefly noted, "It was in the midst of these afflictions and overwhelming engagements that Mr. Fuller, in the year 1800, produced his most celebrated treatise in defence [sic] of the Christian religion" against Deism.[60] Ryland likewise kept his commentary brief, "This is the work of which Mr. Wilberforce spoke so highly, in a letter I received from him just after Mr. Fuller's death."[61] Nonetheless, its innovative argumentation and rich theological basis makes it an important contribution to Evangelical and Baptist ethical thought.

Fuller's Moral Ground of Argument

Fuller found the salutary nature of orthodoxy a compelling ground by which to defend the truth of Christianity against the censure of the Socinians and Deists. He maintained that the doctrines of Calvinism were conducive to virtue, holiness, and happiness. Any compromise of these doctrines led to a compromise in ethics—or, as he put it, "the worst principles will . . . be

---

58. Fuller, *Gospel Its Own Witness*, in *WAF*, 2:7.
59. Ibid., 2:8.
60. A. G. Fuller, *Memoir*, in *WAF*, 1:74.
61. Ryland, *Life and Death of the Rev. Andrew Fuller*, 216.

productive of the worst practices."[62] Motivated chiefly by pastoral sentiments, Fuller was concerned that the abandonment of orthodoxy would lead others further away from the knowledge and love of God and deeper into sinful propensities.

Some have deemed Fuller's ground of argument tenuous. Thomas Belsham disparaged Fuller's approach as jejune elitism, "the amount of it is, 'We Calvinists, being much better Christians than you Socinians, our doctrines must, of course, be true.'"[63] According to Belsham's student, John Kentish, Fuller mistook the worth of a belief for its factuality, "the effects produced by a doctrine were a proper criterion of its value, but not of its truth."[64] Alan Sell joins Fuller's Socinian critics in pronouncing his method to juxtapose the moral tendencies of the respective systems a "hazardous epistemological undertaking." It "must first be granted that Fuller's chosen ground of argument is shaky indeed," Sell claims, judging his attempt "to find exactly the kind of pious experiences and practices . . . that he seeks" a failure. [65] Fuller recognized that his method had its difficulties,[66] but he did not question its epistemic soundness.

In his response to Toulmin, Fuller listed six reasons why he chose to rest the debate on moral grounds. First, comparing the moral tendencies of the respective systems would show which one resembled apostolic doctrine and practice the closest. Second, if a belief tended to virtue, it would corroborate its divine origin. Third, the Scriptures prescribed this method for ascertaining truth and falsehood. The biblical authors summoned believers to test for false teachers and false teaching by their moral fruit.[67] Fourth, Fuller thought that the ingenuity of this method would appeal to public interest. Fifth, the grounds of debate were democratic, open to the judgment of the common people. Most of the writings in the Socinian controversy delved into complicated linguistic and historical issues that catered to the educated—but anyone could observe and gauge a belief system's moral tendencies. Sixth and last, Fuller reminded his readers that the

---

62. Fuller, *Calvinistic and Socinian Systems Examined*, in WAF, 2:149.
63. Quoted in ibid., 2:288.
64. Ibid.
65. Sell, "Andrew Fuller and the Socinians," 135.
66. Fuller, *Calvinistic and Socinian Systems Examined*, in WAF, 2:115.
67. Perhaps Fuller had in mind passages like 2 Pet 2 and Jude 3–16.

Socinians first established the discussion on these grounds in assailing the moral nature of Calvinist belief.[68]

Fuller's defense of orthodoxy on moral grounds was a relatively novel approach in his British context that designated science and reason as the most reliable vehicles for ascertaining truth. As E. F. Clipsham notes, the leading eighteenth-century Christian apologists—such as William Law (1686–1761), Joseph Butler (1692–1754), and William Paley (1743–1805)—imitated their Enlightenment contemporaries in relying on modernist rationalism and Newtonian science to support their claims. Although these thinkers produced masterful apologetic writings, their approach was limited in what it could accomplish, "What it amounted to . . . was an acknowledgement that a special revelation is not improbable, that miracles are not to be dismissed as incredible, and that the light of reason is not so clear and unambiguous as to justify a rejection of Christianity." In the end, their methods were "only able to demonstrate that the balance of probability was in favour of the Christian revelation," but it "had nothing to say about the finality and uniqueness of the gospel, the chief glory of Christianity."[69] Fuller would not settle with merely offering his readers probable truths—rather, he intended to persuade them that the unrivaled goodness and transformative power of the gospel bore witness to its singularity and truthfulness.

Although Fuller's approach struck his contemporaries as unconventional, he had in fact advocated a long-established theological and pastoral notion that the true knowledge and love of God was essential for virtue and happiness. As Ellen Charry argues in her work, *By The Renewing of Your Minds*, "The classic theologians based their understanding of human excellence on knowing and loving God, the imitation of or assimilation to whom brings proper human dignity and flourishing."[70] A brief summary of her argument will help illuminate Fuller's understanding of virtue.

According to Charry, prominent theologians from the apostolic era to the Reformation taught the aretegenic[71] import of the true knowledge of God. Right belief was not merely factual but also salutary. Athanasius of

---

68. Fuller, *Socinianism Indefensible*, in WAF, 2:245.
69. Clipsham, "Fuller and Fullerism," 271–72.
70. Charry, *Renewing of Your Minds*, 18.
71. As explained in the introduction, the term "aretegenic" is a neologism that Charry coined to denote "conducive to virtue." It is a compound derivative from the Greek terms *arete* (virtue) and *gennao* (to beget). Ibid., 19.

Alexandria (c. 299–373) contended against paganism on the basis that beliefs in false gods undermined human worth and morality. God created humans in his image and instructed them in excellence and righteousness, but paganism subverted this good order by encouraging creature-worship and leading people astray from God and his good ways. "By reordering our minds in harmony with the intelligent beauty" of God, Athanasius believed, "we can return to our true selves."[72] Likewise, Augustine of Hippo (354–430) rooted his defense of the doctrine of the Trinity in its salutary nature. Humans find their identity and dignity in knowing the true identity of God, in whose image we exist.[73] The creature must learn truth, justice, wisdom, and joy by knowing God's character.[74] As Charry explains, "A central goal of Augustine's treatise [*De Trinitate*] is to persuade the reader that revelation and doctrine work together to reshape our minds and affections and thereby our identity."[75] Basil of Caesarea (329–379), Anselm of Canterbury (1033–1109), and John Calvin (1509–1564) are among the other theologians Charry examined who promoted orthodox belief with the aretegenic objective of facilitating holiness and virtue through the knowledge of God.

In order to contrast the aretegenic theology of these figures with modernist ethical thought, Charry draws from Augustine's distinction between *scientia* and *sapientia*. *Scientia* concerned knowledge as factuality, and *sapientia* denoted a knowledge that involved wisdom and love. While Augustine considered both forms of knowledge essential, he maintained that the goal of *scientia* was to move the knower to *sapientia*.[76] For Augustine and these other pre-modern theologians, knowledge entailed the affective, aesthetic, and moral participation of the agent—"sapience is engaged knowledge that emotionally connects the knower to the known."[77] Thus, knowing God means to share in his goodness, justice, wisdom, and love.

The modern Academy, Charry claims, has largely reduced knowledge to *scientia*: "Sapiential theology waned with modernity."[78] In the Enlightenment period, "abetted by the epistemology of John Locke," sapience was largely eliminated from the category of truth. Locke forged

72. Ibid., 88–91.
73. Ibid., 147.
74. Ibid., 134–35.
75. Ibid., 133.
76. Ibid.
77. Ibid., 4.
78. Ibid., 5.

an understanding of truth that relied on sensory experience and reason alone, catalyzing the epistemic shift to disjoin "reason from both faith and sapience."[79] Charry summarizes the process of how modern notions of knowledge abandoned sapience:

> Locke separated faith from knowledge, denying the importance of trust as an element of truth. Hume insisted on the repeatability of events as a sign of their truth and disallowed inferential reasoning, tentativeness, and discerning judgment. Kant pointed out that the conditions for knowing lie within the mind itself and that human knowing cannot transcend the limits of time and space within which the mind operates.[80]

Unlike these leaders of modernist philosophy, theologians like Augustine, Anselm, and Calvin "could not envision a notion of truth that is not salutary."[81] The same holds true for Andrew Fuller.[82]

In defending orthodoxy on moral grounds, Fuller sustained the classic theologians' treasured notion of knowledge as *sapientia*. His writings against the Deists and Socinians represent an attempt to preserve not merely the factuality of Christian doctrine but also its aretegenic value. His interlocutors

---

79. Ibid., 7.

80. Ibid., 10.

81. Ibid., 233.

82. Fuller's apologetic approach echoed key aspects of Augustine's defense of Christianity against Roman philosophy and pagan religion in his classic work, *The City of God*. Augustine argued that virtue was inseparable from Christian truth and practice, "no one can possibly have true virtue without true godliness—that is, without the true worship of the true God," for "virtue is not true virtue when it is put to the service of human glory." Augustine, *City of God: Books 1–10*, 172. Augustine defended central Christian doctrines on the basis of their inherent moral goodness. For example, in Book XII he defended God's eternality and immutability against the Platonic notion that history is cyclical rather than linear. Believing that an eternal God created time with both a beginning and an end held enormous import for the Christian's joy. Rather than having to bear through the same cyclical miseries of this world, this doctrine offered hope for eternal happiness with God at the end of time. Only an eternal and immutable God, the creator of time, could provide this hope. Augustine also employed this moral apologetic to defend the Christian belief that God created all of humanity through one man, Adam, as opposed to popular notions of spontaneous generation or that human souls existed eternally. "Nor is there anything more appropriate for human nature to do to counter the vice of contentiousness . . . than to recall our first parent," Augustine wrote, for "God chose to create him as one for the propagation of a multitude precisely for the purpose of admonishing us that we should maintain unity and concord." Christian doctrine furnished motives for justice in humanity. Like Fuller, Augustine held that the salutary nature of Christian belief bore witness to its veracity. Augustine, *City of God: Books 11–22*, XII.21–28, 58–67.

(especially Paine) had participated in the modernist development to eradicate salutarity and sapience from truth by subjecting religious knowledge chiefly to *scientia*. Fuller resisted the modernist epistemic movement by reintroducing the goodness of Christian truth as a credible proof of its verity. Thus, the concession made by Kentish that "the effects produced by a doctrine were a proper criterion of its value" but "not of its truth" was unacceptable to Fuller, who could not sever virtue from truthfulness.[83] Neither could he conceive of the categories suggested by the English poet Anna Barbauld (1743–1825), who observed that some Socinians found Christian doctrine "if not true, at least good to be believed," since "a salutary error is better than a dangerous truth."[84] For Fuller, the moral value of an idea implied its truthfulness: there were only salutary truths, or dangerous errors.

"The Love of God Holds Creation Together": The Basis of Moral Harmony

In the search for a universal standard of morality, the modernists pointed to the ubiquity of reason.[85] The self and its natural faculties furnished humanity with an egalitarian norm for virtue and the capacity to attain it. Fuller did not spurn reason, the benefits of science, or the legitimacy of the human passions, but his understanding of human ability drew a distinction between "reason as *the fitness of things* and reason as *our power or capacity of reasoning*."[86] Unlike his opponents, Fuller believed that the natural human faculties required divine guidance due to the corrupting influence of sin, "I feel my understanding full of darkness, my reason exceedingly imperfect, my will ready to start aside, and my passions strangely volatile." He prayed to God, "teach my reason reason."[87] Although reason was universal, so was moral corruption.

Fuller's understanding of moral inability clashed with the modernists' trust in the goodness of human nature, "Lord Bolingbroke resolves all morality into self-love, as its first principle."[88] By increasing one's love for self,

---

83. Quoted in Fuller, *Calvinistic and Socinian Systems Examined*, in WAF, 2:238.

84. Ibid., 2:152–53.

85. The quote in the subheading is from Fuller, *Gospel Its Own Witness*, in WAF, 2:17.

86. Clipsham, "Fuller and Fullerism," 273. Emphasis original.

87. A. G. Fuller, *Memoir*, in WAF, 1:19.

88. Fuller, *Gospel Its Own Witness*, in WAF, 2:16.

they reasoned, humanity would realize its inherent potential for virtue and happiness. According to Fuller, in declaring the self normative for morality, his opponents had incited discord rather than universal harmony.

> Every new speculator is dissatisfied with the definition of his predecessor, and endeavours to mend it. "Virtue," says Lord Shaftesbury, "is a sense of beauty, of harmony, of order, and proportion, an affection towards the whole of our kind or species." "It is," says Lord Bolingbroke, "only the love of ourselves." "It is every thing that tends to preserve and perfect man," says Volney; and as "good reputation" has this tendency, it is, in his account, "a moral good." "It is whatever is useful in society," says Mr. Hume; and as "health, cleanliness, facility of expression . . ." are of use, they are to be reckoned among the virtues. . . . Mr. Paine brings up the rear, and informs us, "It is doing justice, loving mercy, and . . . endeavouring to make our fellow creatures happy."[89]

The human self with its malleable and conflicting inclinations made it incapable of providing humanity with a uniform rule of morality. "Morality with them is any thing, or nothing, as convenience requires," Fuller concluded.[90]

Despite their diversity in defining morality, these thinkers were united in the belief that God had no active bearing on their ethics. "It is worthy of notice, that, amidst all the discordance of these writers, they agree in excluding the Divine Being from their theory of morals."[91] Fuller listed three common standards that his opponents advocated as regulative for universal morality: the laws of the state, feelings, and the "laws and light of nature."[92] For Fuller, the first two failed to meet the criterion of universality—the laws of the state were inconstant and localized, and human feelings were too capricious. He agreed that the "dictates of nature" were equally "manifest to every man," but natural laws could only expose humanity's moral failures rather than empower men and women in virtue.

> It is one thing to leave sinners without excuse in sin, and another thing to recover them from it. That the light of nature is insufficient for the latter, is demonstrated by melancholy fact. Instead of returning to God and virtue, those nations which have possessed

---

89. Ibid., 2:21.
90. Ibid., 2:20.
91. Ibid., 2:21.
92. Ibid., 2:17–18.

> the highest degrees of it have gone further and further into immorality. . . . Those nations where science diffused a more than ordinary lustre were as superstitious and wicked as the most barbarous, and in many instances exceeded them.[93]

Natural laws failed to restore humanity to virtue not because of any imperfection in nature or reason but because the "judgments of men concerning the dictates of nature are greatly influenced by their prevailing inclinations." Fuller explained, "If under certain circumstances they feel prompted to a particular course of conduct, they will be apt to consider that incitement as a dictate of nature, though it may be no other than corrupt propensity."[94] Due to humanity's moral corruption, natural laws also collapsed as a universally trustworthy rule for virtue.

The love of God alone furnished a reliable standard for virtue. This claim was Fuller's central thesis in his works against the Socinians and Deists. In *The Calvinistic and Socinianism Systems Examined*, he wrote,

> The eternal standard of right and wrong is the moral law, summed up in love to God with all the heart, soul, mind, and strength, and to our neighbour as ourselves. This law is holy, just, and good: holy, as requiring perfect conformity to God; just, as being founded in the strictest equity; and good, as being equally adapted to promote the happiness of the creature and the glory of the Creator.[95]

Only by directing love and glory to God could the creature properly love humanity and achieve genuine happiness. He argued on the same basis in *The Gospel Its Own Witness*.

> The morality which the Scriptures inculcate is summed up in these few words: "Thou shalt love the Lord thy God with all they heart, with all they soul, with all thy mind, with all thy strength; and thy neighbour as thyself." This single principle is competent to the government of all intelligent nature. It is a band that would hold

---

93. Ibid., 2:18–19.
94. Ibid., 2:19.
95. Fuller, *Calvinistic and Socinian Systems Examined*, in *WAF*, 2:137. He's referring to Mark 12:28–31. Fuller wrote, "If Dr. Priestley had formed his estimate of human virtue by that great standard, which requires love to God . . . and to our neighbor . . . instead of representing men by nature as having 'more virtue than vice,' he must have acknowledged with the Scriptures, that . . . 'there is none of them that doeth good, no, not one.'" Ibid., 2:138.

together the whole rational creation, and diffuse peace, order, and happiness wherever it existed.[96]

Unlike the human self or natural laws, the moral law as comprehended in love to God provided humanity with a universal standard for virtue that also held promise to transform corrupt wills.[97]

Fuller primarily derived his understanding of virtue from Jonathan Edwards's work, *The Nature of True Virtue*.[98] For Edwards, "true virtue consists in love to Being in general" as expressed in a "benevolence towards Being."[99] He warned against confusing love and benevolence to particular beings or non-intelligent beings with love to Being in general. "Pure benevolence in its first exercise is nothing else but being's uniting, consent, or propensity to Being; appearing true and pure by its extending to Being in general," and its "inclining to the general highest good, and to each being, whose welfare is consistent with the highest general good, in proportion to the degree of existence."[100] One could only exercise true virtue to another creature if his or her love arose from and conformed to a love to Being in general.

Edwards concluded that since God is "infinitely the greatest and best of beings," true virtue "must chiefly consist in love to God."[101] As the Supreme Being and "head of the universal system of existence," God comprehends

---

96. Fuller, *Gospel Its Own Witness*, in *WAF*, 2:15.

97. The Augustinian voluntarist tradition—which attributed the determining power for belief and morality to the will—was more prominent in the sixteenth and seventeenth centuries, but Fuller seemed to have adopted many of its principles and emphases as mediated through Jonathan Edwards. "In this Augustinian tradition," writes Norman Fiering, "it is love misdirected, not intellectual misjudgment, that is considered the source of moral evil in man." Fiering, *Moral Philosophy at Seventeenth-Century Harvard*, 117. Augustine wrote, "When a person is resolved on loving God and on loving his neighbor as himself, not according to man but according to God, it is undoubtedly on account of this love that he is called a person of good will." Augustine, *City of God*, XIV.7, 106. Fuller's understanding of virtue perpetuated the Augustinian tradition by basing virtue in the love of God and vice in the love of self. Augustine believed that a love for self and a love for God divided men and women into two cities: the earthly city and the heavenly city. Augustine, *City of God*, XIV.28, 136.

98. Edwards, *Nature of True Virtue*, in *WJE*, vol. 8. For more on Edwards's influence on Fuller's ethical thought, see Chun, *Legacy of Jonathan Edwards*, 110–41.

99. Edwards, *Nature of True Virtue*, in *WJE*, 8:541.

100. Ibid., 8:546.

101. Ibid., 8:550.

all beauty, benevolence, excellence, happiness, and goodness.[102] Thus, if one did not first love God, he or she could not truly love other creatures since that love deviated from the ultimate source of love and morality. For Edwards, the problem with "private self-love" was that it terminated on a single person only—it had no regard for being in general and thus no love for God or other creatures. In fact, a person's "personal appetites or private inclinations" that arose from self-love gratified selfish passions alone and were inevitably "inconsistent with the good of the public."[103] On the contrary, "so far as a virtuous mind exercises true virtue in benevolence to created beings, it chiefly seeks the good of the creature, consisting in the knowledge or view of God's glory and beauty, its union with God, and conformity to him, love to him, and joy in him."[104] This last sentence captures Fuller's objective in not only his writings against Priestley and Paine but also in his life and ministry—to return sinners to the love of God by propagating the knowledge of him throughout the earth.

Edwards's influence on Fuller's understanding of virtue is explicit in Fuller's short work entitled "Nature of True Virtue."[105] Similar to Edwards, Fuller defined virtue as love to general being; and since God is the Supreme Being, virtue entailed "to love him supremely, and our fellow creatures in subordination to him."[106] Fuller built upon Edwards's logic more extensively in *The Gospel Its Own Witness*. He wrote, "If mankind loved God supremely, there would be no idolatry upon the earth, nor any of its attendant abominations... no despising of those that are good; no arrogance, ingratitude, pride," and no other evils perpetrated against the Creator and his righteousness.[107] Even more, if humans "loved their fellow creatures as themselves, for his sake, there would be no wars, rivalships, antipathies ... no envyings, strifes, wrongs ... tyranny, venality, haughtiness ... nor murders, robberies," and no other evils committed against humanity.[108] The

---

102. Ibid., 8:551.
103. Ibid., 8:555.
104. Ibid., 8:559.
105. Fuller, "Nature of True Virtue," in *WAF*, 3:817–18. Fuller wrote this tract to answer his friend's objections (Robert Hall) to Edwards's understanding of virtue.
106. Ibid., 3:817.
107. Fuller, *Gospel Its Own Witness*, in *WAF*, 2:16.
108. Ibid.

"love of God holds creation together"; it improved the welfare of society, eradicated evil, and promoted true virtue.[109]

Self-love, on the other hand, was the "source of all the mischief and misery in the universe."[110] Establishing self-love as the source of "moral action" was the same thing as for every individual to treat himself as the Supreme Being.[111] Instead of motivating genuine virtue, self-love undermined love to God and thus love to fellow humanity.

> If our supreme affection terminate on ourselves, and no being, created or uncreated, be regarded but for our own sakes, it is manifest there can be no union beyond the sphere in which other beings become voluntarily subservient to our wishes. The Supreme Being, if our plan do not comport with his, will be continually thwarting us; and so we shall be always at variance with him. And as to create beings, those individuals whom we desire to be subservient to our wishes, having the same right, and the same inclination, to require that we should be subservient to theirs, will also be continually thwarting us; and so we shall always be at variance with them. In short, nothing but an endless succession of discord and confusion can be the consequence.[112]

For Fuller, human beings throughout the centuries have had an ample supply of self-love—it was natural to one's immoral inclinations—and yet self-love had not advanced morality in the least. Thus, self-love was not the solution to moral progress.

Fuller did not despise a love for self as long as it was subordinated to a supreme love for God. He distinguished between a selfish self-love and an unselfish, or disinterested, self-love. The former made the self "the ultimate end of his actions," and it was "mean and mercenary."[113] However, the one who loves his own self disinterestedly "seeks his own well-being in connexion with the general good."[114] Fuller pointed out that the Scriptures called individuals to love their neighbors as themselves. Unlike private self-love, a love for self that was subordinated to love for God advanced love for others. "The nature of heavenly enjoyments is such as to admit of no monopoly,

109. Ibid., 2:17.
110. Ibid.
111. Ibid., 2:16.
112. Ibid., 2:17.
113. Ibid., 2:24.
114. Ibid.

and consequently to leave no room for the exercise of private self-love. . . . The interest of one is the interest of all."¹¹⁵ Only in loving God first can the creature fully experience true love for self and genuine happiness.¹¹⁶

Conclusion

Fuller argued for the truth of Christianity against the Socinians and Deists on the basis of its salutary nature. Since virtue consisted chiefly in the knowledge and love of God, demeaning beliefs about God were subversive to morality. The modernist project to exclude God from notions of virtue and put other moral standards in God's place severely hindered rather than encouraged benevolence and justice. Fuller's goal in defending orthodox doctrines like the Trinity, the atonement, and the veracity of Scriptures was to demonstrate the aretegenic value of the knowledge of God. Christian doctrine was not merely factual but also good and advantageous to the wellbeing of the believer, for its precepts engendered excellence, happiness, and social welfare.

In order to know and love God—and thus know virtue—immoral humanity desperately needed the gospel. Fuller agreed with Edwards that a "man must first love God, or have his heart united to him, before he will esteem God's good his own, and before he will desire the glorifying and enjoying of God, as his happiness."¹¹⁷ The next chapter attempts to systematically present Fuller's theology of virtue, demonstrating how his Evangelical Calvinism provided the framework for his theology of virtue.

---

115. Ibid., 2:25.

116. Many of the New Divinity theologians took Edwards's notions of love for God to "an extreme statement of the doctrine, as if it required a person to be damned if it were God's will." In a letter "to the Rev. Mr. Griffin," Fuller explains that a true love for God necessitated a healthy love for self. Although "Christian hope . . . includes a disinterested affection to the divine character," it did not mean that the we should feel "dead to our best interests" by taking joy in our condemnation if it was God's will. Fuller, "To the Rev. Mr. Griffin," in Haykin, *Armies of the Lamb*, 203–5.

117. Edwards, *Religious Affections*, in *WJE*, 2:241.

4

"A System of Holiness": Fuller's Evangelical Calvinistic Theology of Virtue

FULLER BASED HIS THEOLOGY of virtue on the doctrines that he considered central to the gospel.[1] The truth and import of Evangelical beliefs about the righteous character of God, the depravity of humanity, the deity and atonement of Christ, and the veracity of Scripture rested in their aretegenic power to convert moral agents from evil and instill in them holiness and love. This chapter will discuss how Fuller's Evangelical Calvinist doctrines shaped his theology of virtue. For Fuller, the clash between good and evil did not consist merely in rival philosophical axioms; rather, it took place in a cosmic drama in which every moral agent was personally involved. In order to depict the dynamic between God's moral authority and humanity's moral insubordination, Fuller employed the analogy of a government. God was like a moral governor who in his love desired to find a means to pardon the rebels without compromising his justice.

---

1. An earlier version of this chapter was published as "'A System of Holiness': Andrew Fuller's Evangelical Calvinistic Theology of Virtue," in *Puritan and Reformed Journal* 6 (2014) 123–45, and is reprinted here by gracious permission of the editors of the journal. The quote in the chapter title is from Fuller, *Calvinistic and Socinian Systems Examined*, in *WAF*, 2:134.

Fuller's Evangelical Theology and the Moral Order

In his engagement with Socinianism, Andrew Fuller outlined the "principal objections to the Calvinistic system" with regard to the atonement, the glory of God, and "the worship paid to Jesus Christ" as fully God.[2] The Deists censured the same doctrines but also included an aggressive opposition to the truth of Scripture. Fuller's aim in both polemical contests was to show that the salutary nature of these doctrines bore witness to their veracity.

Fuller considered each doctrine of Evangelical Calvinist theology crucial to maintaining the moral order. To negate just one belief undermined the harmony of not only truth but also of moral goodness. "There is such a connexion in truth, that, if one part of it be given up, it will render us less friendly towards other parts, and so destroy their efficacy."[3] Joseph Priestley confessed belief in the resurrection but denied Christ's deity and atonement. Paine held to the doctrine of a future life, but he rejected Scripture and challenged the goodness of the Christian God. Fuller countered that his opponents' moral system was incomplete because their belief system was incomplete. The truth of a belief system and its aretegenic value stood and fell together, for "that which we account truth is a system of holiness."[4] Hence, he believed that if he could display "the morality and virtue inculcated by the gospel," then he could corroborate the truthfulness of its doctrines.[5] The following pages delineate the way Fuller's theological system shaped his moral worldview.

"The Prime Object of Genuine Love": The God of Moral Glory

In *The Gospel Its Own Witness*, Fuller commenced his moral argumentation with the doctrine of God.[6] God's holy character furnished the standard and source of virtue. He wrote, "There are certain perfections which all

---

2. Fuller, *Calvinistic and Socinian Systems Examined*, in WAF, 2:154.
3. Fuller, *Gospel Its Own Witness*, in WAF, 2:23.
4. Fuller, *Calvinistic and Socinian Systems Examined*, in WAF, 2:134.
5. Fuller, *Gospel Its Own Witness*, in WAF, 2:14.
6. The quote in the subheading is from Fuller, *Calvinistic and Socinian Systems Examined*, in WAF, 2:153–54.

who acknowledge a God agree in attributing to him; such are those of wisdom, power, immutability, &c." These attributes constitute God's natural perfections. "There are others which no less evidently belong to Deity," Fuller explained, "such as goodness, justice, veracity, &c., all which may be expressed in one word—holiness." Fuller counted these traits among God's moral perfections. Although both "natural and moral attributes tend to display the glory of the Divine character," Fuller claimed that God's moral perfections exhibited his glory far greater than his natural perfections. A person's greatness will win acclaim, but a person's goodness will captivate hearts. He wrote, "Moral excellence is the highest glory of any intelligent being, created or uncreated. Without this, wisdom would be subtlety, power tyranny, and immutability the same thing as being unchangeably wicked." Thus, although natural perfections like wisdom and power render God's character "a proper object of admiration," his "justice, veracity, and goodness attract our love" and capture our devotion.[7]

According to Fuller, the religions of the world have largely overlooked the divine moral character. The pagans have fabricated deities that represent greatness and power; but when it came to the moral character of their idols—many of which stood for drunkenness, sexual promiscuity, human sacrifice, and deception—they fell considerably short. The Deists emphasized God's natural perfections, praising his transcendent grandeur, might, and intelligence while often ignoring his moral character. Fuller accused both the pagans and Deists alike of imposing their moral norms on their conception of the divine.[8] In contrast, the moral character of God determined Christian belief and its understanding of virtue. "The object of Christian adoration is Jehovah, the God of Israel; whose character for holiness, justice, and goodness, is displayed in the doctrines and precepts of the gospel."[9] The gospel represented not merely a solution for humanity's moral problem—it revealed the moral glory of God.

Fuller's defense of the Evangelical doctrine of God against the accusations of vindictiveness and malevolence was driven by his aretegenic goal to promote virtue in his readers. Human beings learned virtue by knowing God, practiced virtue by obeying God, and loved virtue by loving God. Fuller believed that a "cordial approbation of the Divine character is the same thing as a disinterested affection to virtue." Even more, a "holy

7. Fuller, *Gospel Its Own Witness*, in *WAF*, 2:9.
8. Ibid., 2:13.
9. Ibid., 2:9.

likeness to God" was equivalent to "the very practice or exercise of virtue."[10] Thus, Fuller deemed it impossible to grow in correct moral thinking and conduct without having accurate beliefs about and affection for God's good character and ways.

> It is the character of God that is the prime object of genuine love. . . . The true character of God, as revealed in the Scriptures, must be taken into account, in determining whether our love to God be genuine or not. We may clothe the Divine Being with such attributes, and such only, as will suit our depraved taste; and then it will be no difficult thing to fall down and worship him: but this is not the love of God, but an idol of our own creating.[11]

Fuller perceived that one's knowledge of God's moral character spoke volumes about his or her own character and moral standards. He charged his opponents with adapting their doctrine of God to their love of self. Their commitment to God was ultimately an "attachment to a being whose glory consists in his being invariably attached to us."[12] The irony of making God subservient to the creature's inclinations was that it divested God of his power to benefit humanity and facilitate its morality and happiness. The god of Enlightenment religion played no role in reforming humanity's moral practices and ideas but merely existed to endorse them. Fuller argued that excluding the Christian God from morality was not only ideologically flawed but it also undermined the advancement of virtue.

In Fuller's moral cosmology, God's moral glory comprehended the nature and beauty of virtue. God held the "supreme place in the system of being," and his being was the source of all creation's existence.[13] Likewise, his good character occupied the supreme place in the moral system, and therefore all goodness in creation originated in him. Thus, Fuller concluded that the best vehicle for becoming a person of virtue was to assign all glory and worship to God as the Supreme Being.

> The great God, who fills heaven and earth, must be allowed to form the far greatest proportion, if I may so speak, of the whole system of being; for, compared with him, "all nations," yea, all worlds, "are but as a drop of a bucket, or as the small dust of the balance." He is the source and continual support of existence, in all

---

10. Ibid., 2:25.
11. Fuller, *Calvinistic and Socinian Systems Examined*, in WAF, 2:153–54.
12. Fuller, *Socinianism Indefensible*, in WAF, 2:270.
13. Fuller, *Calvinistic and Socinian Systems Examined*, in WAF, 2:159.

> its varied forms. As the great Guardian of being in general, therefore, it is fit and right that he should, in the first place, guard the glory of his own character and government. Nor can this be to the disadvantage of the universe, but the contrary; as it will appear, if it be considered that it is the glory of God to do that which shall be best upon the whole. The glory of God, therefore, connects with it the general good of the created system, and of all its parts, except those whose welfare clashes with the welfare of the whole.[14]

The ultimate objective of creation rested in ascribing worship, love, and obedience to the God of moral glory. Fuller perceived that the supremacy of God's moral glory in creation held clear implications for human virtue. "That place which God holds in the great system of being he ought to hold in our affections; for we are not required to love him in a greater proportion than the place which he occupies requires."[15] When human beings make God the object of their affections, they will imitate his goodness and live in moral harmony with creation.

Fuller's aretegenic objective to advance the universal welfare of humanity drove his defense of the Calvinist notion of God against its critics. God was no vindictive egotist to promote his glory as primary and require creation to do likewise, for it is "thus that the love of God holds creation together." For Fuller, the glory of God provided creation with its universal unifying principle. "He is that lovely character to whom all holy intelligences bear supreme affection; and the display of his glory, in the universal triumph of truth and righteousness, is that end which they all pursue." In order for true social justice, compassion, and freedom to prevail universally, humanity needed to find solidarity in an ultimate telos to glorify and love God. "Thus united in their grand object they cannot but feel a union of heart with one another."[16] Thus, in promoting the glory of God, human beings not only learned to love God but also their neighbor.

God's character embodied goodness, love, and righteousness—thus, to establish his moral glory as supreme resulted in creation's greatest well-being. If God substituted his moral glory for another standard as the end of creation, then true virtue would be eclipsed.

> If it were otherwise, if the happiness of all creatures were the great end that God from the beginning had in view, then, doubtless, in

---

14. Ibid., 2:159–60.
15. Ibid., 2:159.
16. Fuller, *Gospel Its Own Witness*, in WAF, 2:15.

> order that this end might be accomplished, every thing else must, as occasion required, give way to it. The glory of his own character, occupying only a subordinate place in the system, if ever it should stand in the way of that which is supreme, must give place, among other things. And if God have consented to all this, it must be because the happiness, not only of creation in general, but of every individual, is an object of the greatest magnitude, and most fit to be chosen; that is, it is better, and more worthy of God, as the Governor of the universe, to give up his character for purity, equity, wisdom, and veracity, and to become vile and contemptible in the eyes of his creatures—it is better that the bands which bind all holy intelligences to him should be broken, and the cords which hold together the whole moral system be cast away than that the happiness of a creature should, in any instance, be given up![17]

Fuller set this point against Priestley's criticism that Calvinists disregarded the happiness of humanity in asserting the glory of God as the supreme end of virtue. "'Those who assume to themselves the distinguishing title of orthodox,' says Dr. Priestley, 'consider the Supreme Being as having created all things for his glory, and by no means for the general happiness of all his creatures.'" Fuller responded that Priestley sorely misrepresented Calvinists, for creatures find true happiness in glorifying God first and foremost. Even more, Fuller objected that human notions of happiness are often selfish and would not benefit the good of the whole, making it a deficient standard of morality. If God's ultimate objective was to promote the creature's happiness over his glory, Fuller reasoned, then God has so far been immensely unsuccessful, since "All creatures, we are certain, are not happy in this world."[18]

God held an infinitely greater place in the system of being than everything else; therefore, his moral glory was paramount. If God allowed sinful humanity to determine the standard of virtue and assert its warped notions of happiness as the supreme end of creation, then he would fail as a moral judge over evil. Even more, he would fail to benefit his creation, for the "glory of God consists . . . in doing that which is best upon the whole."[19] Contrary to the objections of Fuller's opponents, God acted for the good

---

17. Fuller, *Calvinistic and Socinian Systems Examined*, in WAF, 2:160.
18. Ibid., 2:158.
19. Ibid.

and happiness of creation in establishing his moral glory as the supreme object of adoration and emulation.[20]

God expressed his moral perfections in his moral law. Fuller designated the moral law as "the eternal standard of right and wrong," which was "summed up in love to God with all the heart, soul, mind, and strength, and to our neighbour as ourselves."[21] The moral law grounded all of God's precepts—he never issued a commandment that did not brim with his love and goodwill. Like God's moral character, the moral law was eternal and thus set above the volatile moral standards that finite humanity has invented. The aretegenic value of the moral law consisted in its intention to establish righteous relationships between God and human beings and foster social justice and love between neighbors. Fuller argued that the order of the moral law was crucial to its efficacy. Without first loving God, it was impossible to love one's neighbor and treat him or her with dignity. The moral law also existed as a standard to judge evil. Every evil action had its source in an absence of love to God, which was the same as an absence of love to virtue itself.

Since the moral law was an extension of God's moral character, any deviation from it merited God's righteous judgment.

> If the moral law require love to God with all the heart, and soul, and mind, and strength, and to our neighbour as ourselves, it cannot allow the least degree of alienation of the heart from God, or the smallest instance of malevolence to man. And if it be what the Scripture says it is, holy, just, and good, then, though it require all the heart, and soul, and mind, and strength, it cannot be too strict; and if it be not too strict, it cannot be unworthy of God, nor can it be "merciless tyranny" to abide by it.[22]

---

20. Fuller followed Edwards's reasoning in his treatise, *Concerning the End for which God Created the World*. Edwards wrote, "If God in himself be in any respect properly capable of being his own end in the creation of the world, then it is reasonable to suppose that he had respect to himself as his last and highest end in this work; because he is worthy in himself to be so, being infinitely the greatest and best of beings. . . . And therefore if God esteems, values, and has respect to things according to their nature and proportions, he must necessarily have the greatest respect to himself. . . . To him belongs the whole of the respect that any moral agent, either God or any intelligent being, is capable of. To him belongs all the heart." Fuller agreed that moral agents realize their chief end and greatest happiness in knowing, loving, and glorifying God. Edwards, *End for which God Created the World*, in *WJE*, 8:421–22. For more on this work, see Marsden, *Jonathan Edwards*, 459–63.

21. Fuller, *Calvinistic and Socinian Systems Examined*, in *WAF*, 2:137.

22. Ibid., 2:138.

The Love of God Holds Creation Together

God was no tyrant to hold creation accountable to his standard of moral justice. In guarding his glory and moral character, God maintained moral order and promoted the general good of the universe. Thus, God administered his judgments for the benefit of creation, not its injury.

Defending God from the charge of unwarranted vindictiveness, Fuller wrote,

> God ... in the punishment of sin, is not to be considered as acting in a merely private capacity, but as the universal moral Governor; not as separate from the great system of being, but as connected with it, or as the Head and Guardian of it. Now, in this relation, vindictive justice is not only consistent with the loveliness of his character, but essential to it. Capacity and inclination to punish disorder in a state are never thought to render an earthly prince less lovely in the eyes of his loyal and faithful subjects, but more so.[23]

Here Fuller was directly responding to Priestley's claim that Calvinists "represent God in such a light that no earthly parent could imitate him, without sustaining a character shocking to mankind."[24] Priestley argued that this notion of a judging God did not make him imitable and worthy of love. Fuller countered that God's judgments were ultimately directed for the good of the whole and were therefore justified. God would in fact be far more malevolent if he allowed evil free reign. God as the Supreme Being and protector of the ultimate good not only possessed the right but also the moral responsibility to judge evil. A God who did not exercise justice would be "neither loved nor feared, but would become the object of universal contempt."[25] Only when moral agents acknowledge God's moral glory can they understand his equity and goodness in judging sinners.

"The Grand Succedaneum": Humanity's Moral Slavery to Self-Love

Fuller attributed considerable aretegenic value to the doctrine of human depravity.[26] Since Christian belief held a correct estimation of humanity's moral state, it alone could offer a remedy. In fact, the reality of universal

---

23. Ibid., 2:157–58.
24. Ibid., 2:155.
25. Fuller, *Gospel Its Own Witness*, in *WAF*, 2:10.
26. The quote in the subheading is from Fuller, *Dialogues and Letters Between Crispus and Gaius*, in *WAF*, 2:662.

corruption attested to the truth of Christianity. "This single principle of human depravity, supposing it to be true, will fully account for all the moral disorders in the world," and "the actual existence of those disorders, unless they can be better accounted for, must go to prove the truth of this principle, and, by consequence, of the Christian system which rests upon it."[27] As long as human beings continued in the delusion that their desires, passions, and conduct were not sinful but inherently good, they could never turn from evil to the love of God. Therefore, "the system which affords the most enlarged views of the evil of sin must needs have the greatest tendency to promote repentance for it."[28] The doctrine of human depravity possessed singular power to inspire human beings to resist and turn from evil by exposing them to sin's heinousness.

According to Fuller, the Scriptures taught that the "spring-head whence all the malignant streams of idolatry, atheism, corruption, persecution, war, and every other evil" lay in humanity's refusal to devote its love supremely to God.[29] The absence of love for God not only introduced sin into the world but it has sustained it ever since.

> It has already been observed, that Christian morality is summed up in the love of God and our neighbour, and that these principles, carried to their full extent, would render the world a paradise. But the Scriptures teach us that man is a rebel against his Maker; that his carnal mind is enmity against God, and is not subject to the law of God, neither indeed can be; that instead of loving God, or even man, in the order which is required, men are become "lovers of their own selves," and neither God nor man is regarded but as they are found necessary to subserve their wishes.[30]

As the "sum of the Divine law is love," Fuller concluded that the "essence of depravity" consisted "in the want of love to God and neighbor."[31] The object of a person's love determined his or her conformity to the moral law.

Fuller imputed all moral rebellion to the love of self.

> All objects set up in competition with God and our neighbour may be reduced to one, and that is *self*. Private self-love seems to be the root of depravity; the grand succedaneum in human

27. Fuller, *Gospel Its Own Witness*, in WAF, 2:65.
28. Fuller, *Calvinistic and Socinian Systems Examined*, in WAF, 2:116.
29. Fuller, *Gospel Its Own Witness*, in WAF, 2:64.
30. Ibid.
31. Fuller, *Dialogues and Letters Between Crispus and Gaius*, in WAF, 2:662.

> affections to the love of God and man. Self-admiration, self-will, and self-righteousness are but different modifications of it. Where this prevails, the creature assumes the place of the Creator, and seeks his own gratification, honour, and interest, as the ultimate end of all his actions.[32]

The preoccupation with self-love has hampered rather than hastened the development of human virtue. First and foremost, it eroded and undermined a supreme love for God. Without a love for God, an agent could not have a sincere understanding of and affection for virtue. It also has blinded humanity to its evil. When the self is adored and served as paramount, a person cannot form an accurate opinion about the justice of his or her own character, ideas, and ways. A love of self has inspired creatures to estimate their moral nature according to their own standards rather than by God's moral law. And it not only made creatures hostile to their Creator but also to their neighbors. A person's inclinations drive all of his or her actions, even if such inclinations appear benevolent and loving on the surface. If an agent's motivation was not chiefly the love of God, his or her actions were not in agreement with real virtue.

Fuller understood innate depravity to entail the enslavement of all of humanity under the rule of sin. The human will held no power to reform wickedness because the corrupt will was the very thing that enslaved human beings to sin in the first place. Many Enlightenment thinkers lambasted the Calvinist doctrine of innate depravity because it diminished the moral agent's freedom, but Fuller flipped the charge on its head. "Moral slavery, any more than moral liberty, has nothing to do with free agency. The reason is, that, in this case, there is no force opposed to the agent's own will."[33] Every human being was under the dominion of his or her most dominant inclinations. Thus, when an agent's will rejected God's moral law and inclined toward selfishness, the moral slavery involved was voluntary and self-imposed. No one could be virtuous because no one desired God, the standard and giver of virtue.

Humanity had rebelled against God because his moral character was "not suited to their inclinations."[34] In the place of God, humanity fabricated objects of adoration that gratified their selfish inclinations. "If men be destitute of the love of God, it is natural to suppose they will endeavour

32. Ibid. Emphasis original.
33. Ibid., 2:656.
34. Fuller, *Gospel Its Own Witness*, in WAF, 2:10.

to banish him from their thoughts . . . substituting gods more congenial with their inclinations."[35] God's holiness and righteousness did not appeal to the wicked. Human beings perceived God's moral character as a threat to fulfilling their selfish desires, and as a result they projected their depraved inclinations on their self-made idols. "If we be enemies to moral excellence, God, as a holy Being, will possess no loveliness in our eyes," Fuller wrote, and "the further his moral character is kept out of sight, the more agreeable it will be to us."[36] All attempts to accommodate the moral character of God to human inclinations were ultimately rooted in contempt for moral goodness.

"Love of God Wrought in a Way of Righteousness": Christ's Moral Atonement

Fuller regarded the doctrine of the cross as "the central point in which all the lines of evangelical truth meet and are united."[37] Christ's atonement held Fuller's theology of virtue together, offering the single greatest demonstration of divine justice and goodness. His opponents could not have disagreed more.

> The doctrine of atonement, as held by the Calvinists, is often represented by Dr. Priestley as detracting from the goodness of God, and as inconsistent with his natural placability. He seems always to consider this doctrine as originating in the want of love . . . as though God could not find in his heart to show mercy without a price being paid for it.[38]

Paine likewise disputed the morality of the atonement.

> Moral justice cannot take the innocent for the guilty. . . . To suppose justice to do this is to destroy the principle of its existence. . . . It is no longer justice. It is indiscriminate revenge.[39]

These Enlightenment thinkers rejected the atonement on the basis of their beliefs about God and human nature. They represented humanity as

---

35. Ibid., 2:65.
36. Ibid., 2:10.
37. Fuller, *Calvinistic and Socinian Systems Examined*, in *WAF*, 2:182. The quote in the subheading is from ibid., 2:154.
38. Ibid., 2:154.
39. Paine, *Age of Reason*, 285.

inherently moral and God as placid and rational—therefore, God had no need to judge humanity or an innocent substitute in its place.

Fuller determined the morality of the atonement by a completely different anthropology and doctrine of God.

> Those who embrace the Calvinistic system believe that man was originally created holy and happy; that of his own accord he departed from God, and became vile; that God, being in himself infinitely amiable, deserves to be, and is, the moral centre of the intelligent system; that rebellion against him is opposition to the general good; that, if suffered to operate according to its tendency, it would destroy the well-being of the universe, by excluding God, and righteousness, and peace, from the whole system; that seeing it aims destruction at universal good, and tends to universal anarchy and mischief, it is, in those respects, an infinite evil, and deserving of endless punishment; and that, in whatever instance God exercises forgiveness, it is not without respect to that public expression of his displeasure against it which was uttered in the death of his Son.[40]

All of humanity voluntarily exchanged the love of God and virtue for their immoral passions. God as the sovereign judge of the universe and guardian of righteousness must execute justice on their evil rebellion. Without the cross, Fuller maintained, sinful humanity had no hope for virtue and thus no escape from God's righteous judgment. Fuller's aretegenic motive to defend and promote belief in Christ's atonement was to restore sinners to the love of God and to offer humanity hope for righteousness and moral excellence. He passionately defended the doctrine of the cross because it summoned humanity to rely on God entirely for virtue.

In order to communicate the gravity and moral significance of the atonement, Fuller presented the doctrine in terms of a cosmic governmental drama.[41] In *The Gospel Its Own Witness*, Fuller employed a governmen-

---

40. Fuller, *Calvinistic and Socinian Systems Examined*, in WAF, 2:116.

41. Among the most controversial aspects of Fuller's theology is his appropriation of governmental language when describing the atonement. The Dutch jurist Hugo Grotius (1583–1645) first articulated the governmental theory of the atonement, and many of Jonathan Edwards's disciples who led the New Divinity Movement—like Joseph Bellamy (1719–1790), Samuel Hopkins (1721–1803), Stephen West (1735–1819), and Jonathan Edwards Jr. (1745–1801)—had adopted it as a central aspect of their theology. Fuller digested the New Divinity writings and even had regular correspondence with some of them. Many have debated whether Edwards himself held the theory. I agree with Oliver Crisp that although Edwards had clear differences with the

tal illustration to prove that the use of a mediator was consistent with sober reason. "Let us suppose," Fuller wrote, "a division of the army of one of the wisest and best of kings . . . traitorously conspired against his crown and life."[42] The empire naturally expected the king to punish the traitors, but the king loved the men and desired to extend mercy. However, the king faced a dilemma as to how he could simultaneously show mercy and maintain moral justice. "'To make light of the controversy,' the king said to his friends, 'would loosen the bands of good government.'"[43] The only solution was to find a mediator who met these unique qualifications: he could not have participated in the offence, he must be highly esteemed by both the king and the public, the degree of the mediation must amount to the

---

New Divinity take on the atonement, it seems that he may have sown the seeds. Crisp, "Moral Government of God," 78–90.

The governmental theory of the atonement teaches that sin consists in rebellion against the moral governor of the universe. In order to maintain his honor as well as the balance of justice in the cosmos, God as the moral governor must execute punishment on the guilty. However, the righteous moral governor is a God of love, and he thus desires to find a way to exercise grace and pardon the guilty without compromising his justice. The solution was to make a grand display of his righteous aversion to sin by punishing the innocent Christ. For more on the New Divinity articulation of this doctrine, see Foster, *Genetic History*, 107–269; and Sweeney, *Nathaniel Taylor*.

Crisp demonstrates two key differences between Edwards Sr. and the New Divinity on the atonement that could also be said for Fuller. First, Edwards "conceives of the atonement as definite and limited in scope." Second, "Edwards clearly endorses the doctrine of penal substitution," an "idea that is abandoned by the representatives of the New Divinity." Crisp, "Moral Government of God," 84–85. Like Edwards, Fuller affirmed the doctrines of limited atonement and penal substitution. Thus, Fuller more than likely derived his articulation of the atonement mainly from Edwards and not the New Divinity.

Chris Chun suggests that Fuller employed governmental language antecedent to his correspondence with the New Divinity theologians. A hand-written draft of *Gospel Worthy of All Acceptation* (a text that employs much governmental language) was recently discovered and could date back to 1778. Chun notes that Fuller's connection with the New Divinity men did not commence until the 1790s. Thus, Fuller was likely indebted more to Edwards or other sources for his use of governmental language rather than to the New Divinity men, which explains why he did not compromise limited atonement and particular redemption. Chun, *The Legacy of Jonathan Edwards in the Theology of Andrew Fuller*, 182. For more on the subject, see Haykin, "Particular Redemption in the Writings of Andrew Fuller," 122–38.

Most treatments of Fuller's use of governmental language have focused on its role in his soteriology. The aim of this study is not to highlight the historical and theological issues surrounding the debate but rather to show how he harnessed the image to present his moral worldview in his Enlightenment context.

42. Fuller, *Gospel Its Own Witness*, in *WAF*, 2:76.

43. Ibid.

weight of the crime, he must have compassion for the guilty, and he must have a close relationship with the king in order to fully display the king's determination to uphold morality in offering mercy.[44] After deliberating with his counselors as to whom in the kingdom could meet these qualifications, the king sought the advice of his son.

> "My son!" said the benevolent sovereign, "what can be done in behalf of these unhappy men? To order them for execution violates every feeling of my heart; yet to pardon them is dangerous. The army, and even the empire, would be under a strong temptation to think lightly of rebellion. If mercy be exercised, it must be through a mediator; and who is qualified to mediate in such a cause? And what expedient can be devised by means of which pardon shall not relax, but strengthen just authority?"[45]

The prince responded, "I feel the insult offered to your person and government.... They have transgressed without cause, and deserve to die without mercy. Yet I also feel for them." The prince thus offered the only possible solution: "On me be this wrong!" Motivated by love for the king, for the criminals, and for righteousness, the innocent prince volunteered to take the punishment on behalf of the guilty. "Inflict on me as much as is necessary to impress the army and nation with a just sense of the evil, and of the importance of good order and faithful allegiance." The king, full of sorrow and love for the prince yet satisfied at his courage, accepted the offer. "Go, my son, assume the likeness of a criminal, and suffer in their place!"[46]

At first, the criminals remained incorrigible, resistant to the king's extension of pardon and reconciliation. But the justness and grace of the king and the goodness of the prince ultimately won their allegiance. "The dignity of his character, together with his surprising condescension and goodness, impresses us more than anything else, and fills our hearts with penitence, confidence, and love ... we are utterly unworthy."[47] The criminals enjoyed a new devotion and affection for the king because they recognized their complete unworthiness of his love. Even more, they honored the king because even though he loved and pardoned the guilty, he did not compromise his justice. The mediation of the prince alone made this

---

44. Ibid., 2:76–77.
45. Ibid., 2:77.
46. Ibid.
47. Ibid., 2:79.

reconciliation possible: it manifested the king's love, satisfied his justice, and restored the rebels to righteousness.

The main goal of this illustration was to highlight the importance of Christ's atonement for maintaining moral order. In upholding the righteousness of God, the atonement caused justice to triumph over evil. It counteracted the forces of the wicked to undermine the moral system by bearing the guilt of the world. It was designed to advance the well-being of the whole and the good of the public by promoting love, reconciliation, and moral justice. The atonement thus displayed "*the love of God wrought in a way of righteousness.*"[48] It was God's "appointed medium" to pour "forth all the fullness of his heart."[49] For Fuller, God did not need the atonement in order to love sinners. Rather, he required a sacrifice for sins due to his goodness—it was necessary in order to preserve the equity of moral government. "Receiving them to favour without some public expression of displeasure against their sin would have been a dishonour to his government" and to the moral order of the universe.[50] As the moral governor, God could not compromise his righteousness when extending his love to sinful creatures.

> The incapacity of God to show mercy without an atonement, is no other than that of a righteous governor, who, whatever good-will he may bear to an offender, cannot admit the thought of passing by the offence, without some public expression of his displeasure against it; that, while mercy triumphs, it may not be at the expense of law and equity, and of the general good.[51]

Contrary to the objections of Paine and Priestley, belief in the atonement was not inconsistent with the love of God. Fuller affirmed that love and justice must co-exist, and he charged his opponents with sacrificing the goodness of God at the expense of his love in abandoning the doctrine of the atonement.

Moreover, Fuller stressed that Christ's atonement satisfied moral rather than commercial justice.[52] He believed that Paine had misrepresented the

---

48. Fuller, *Calvinistic and Socinian Systems Examined*, in *WAF*, 2:154. Emphasis original.

49. Ibid.

50. Ibid., 2:155.

51. Ibid., 2:154.

52. Fuller initially expressed this position in *The Gospel Worthy of All Acceptation*: "the atonement of Christ" proceeded "not on the principle of commercial, but of moral

morality of the atonement by claiming that it had "for its basis an idea of pecuniary justice, and not that of moral justice." Paine reasoned thus: "If I owe a person money, and cannot pay him, and he threatens to put me into prison, another person can take the debt upon himself . . . but if I have committed a crime, every circumstance of the case is changed."[53] In reply, Fuller explained that when Scripture described sin as a debt, it referred to what the sinner owed God by way of moral duty—not a commercial payment. Since every agent owed moral obedience to the supreme moral governor, humanity's disobedience and sin created its moral debt. Thus, sinners did not require an economic payment in order to satisfy the governor but a moral reckoning. "As sin is not a pecuniary, but a moral debt, so the atonement for it is not pecuniary, but a moral ransom."[54] Fuller thought that the governmental analogy better elucidated the moral nature of the sinners' debt and Christ's atonement than the commercial imagery. The prince's death was not a commercial transaction but a moral redemption. By taking the punishment for the rebels' moral disobedience in their stead, he atoned for their moral debt and satisfied the king's "moral justice."[55]

Whether one rendered the atonement on the basis of pecuniary or moral justice was important to moral order, Fuller argued. The moral atonement maintained the justice of God in extending mercy to the guilty. According to Fuller, a commercial payment downplayed the personal dimension of both the offence and the mercy in the pardon.

> Redemption by Jesus Christ was accomplished, not by a satisfaction that should preclude the exercise of grace in forgiveness, but in which, the displeasure of God against sin being manifested, mercy to the sinner might be exercised without any suspicion of his having relinquished his regards for righteousness.[56]

A commercial atonement "excludes the idea of *free* pardon on the part of the creditor, and admits of a *claim* on the part of the debtor," but "it is otherwise in relation to crimes."[57] Fuller insisted on expressing the atonement in moral rather than commercial terms because it held greater aretegenic

---

justice, or justice as it relates to crime." Fuller, *Gospel Worthy of All Acceptation*, in *WAF*, 2:373.

53. Paine, *Age of Reason*, 285.
54. Fuller, *Gospel Its Own Witness*, in *WAF*, 2:80.
55. Ibid., 2:81.
56. Ibid., 2:82.
57. Ibid., 2:81.

weight—it called criminals to not "come before him as claimants, but as supplicants, imploring mercy in the mediator's name."[58] The moral nature of the atonement emphasized the evilness of the debt and the judiciousness of the pardon. The goodness, equity, and grace of the moral atonement were ultimately what stirred the criminals to renounce evil and love the king. "Divine love is the cause, the first cause of our salvation, and of the death of Christ, to that end."[59]

Fuller also contended that the divine character of Christ was essential to the success of his moral atonement. "Let it be inquired," said Fuller, "whether this great end of moral government could have been answered by the sufferings of a mere creature." In Fuller's moral cosmology, no upright human being could satisfy God's moral displeasure against a world of criminals, for "an atonement must be of so much account in the scale of being as to attract the general attention."[60] Christ's divine nature uniquely qualified him to effect atonement for the guilty, for he occupied the same space of being as the Father. Contrary to his opponents, Fuller deemed belief in the deity of Christ as necessary for morality. Humanity had the moral duty to love and worship Christ because he possessed all the same divine natural and moral perfections as the Father.

> Further, It ought to be considered that, in worshipping the Son of God, we worship him not on account of that wherein he differs from the Father, but on account of those perfections which we believe him to possess in common with him. This, with the consideration that we worship him not to the exclusion of the Father, any more than the Father to the exclusion of him, but as one with him, removes all apprehensions from our minds that, in ascribing glory to the one, we detract from that of the other.[61]

Since the Son partook in the divine nature, no mortal could question the equity of his satisfaction of the Father's justice. As Fuller reasoned, "the satisfaction of justice in all cases of offence requires" a punishment "equal to what the nature of the offence is in reality."[62] If any other creature could have "satisfied justice," or if "any gift from the Divine Father, short of that of his only begotten Son, would have answered the great purposes of moral government," then

---

58. Ibid., 2:82.
59. Fuller, *Calvinistic and Socinian Systems Examined*, in WAF, 2:154.
60. Fuller, *Deity of Christ*, in WAF, 3:694.
61. Fuller, *Calvinistic and Socinian Systems Examined*, in WAF, 2:161.
62. Fuller, *The Deity of Christ*, in WAF, 3:694.

"there is no reason to think that he could have made him a sacrifice, but would have spared him, and not freely have 'delivered him up for us all.'"[63] In order to attract attention to the Father's display of his justice and love, the Son of God himself had to become a creature and rectify the moral order. Thus, belief in the deity of Christ was critical to moral virtue.

The doctrine of the atonement instructed humanity in justice, grace, love, and humility. According to Fuller, the world rejected the atonement because the doctrine questioned human ability to achieve virtue. It especially challenged human pride to rely on a mediator for goodness.

> It is far less humbling for an offender to be pardoned at his own request than through the interposition of a third person; for, in the one case, he may be led to think that it was his virtue and penitence which influenced the decision; whereas, in the other, he is compelled to feel his own unworthiness: and this may be one reason why the mediation of Christ is so offensive. It is no wonder, indeed, that those who deny humility to be a virtue should be disgusted with a doctrine the professed object of which is to abase the pride of man.[64]

Fuller regarded humility as essential to virtue. Criminals have no moral ability to redeem themselves—everyone was enslaved to their immoral inclinations and had no personal righteousness to rest on. Belief in the atonement summoned moral agents to humble themselves, renounce their self-love, admit their guilt, and depend on Christ for morality. As Augustine put it, "the more the human soul sets its heart on temporal and mutable things, the more it is unlike the incorporeal, eternal, and immutable being. To heal this condition, since it is impossible for the mortal and impure things here below to approach the immortal purity on high, a mediator is obviously needed."[65]

In sum, belief in the gospel alone made virtue possible. "The only method by which the rewards of the gospel are attainable, faith in Christ, secures the exercise of disinterested and enlarged virtue."[66] Its doctrines enjoined repentance from moral evil and faith in Christ for righteousness. Fuller defined repentance as "a change of mind. It arises from a conviction that we have been in the wrong; and consists in holy shame, grief,"

---

63. Ibid., 3:695. He cited Rom 8:32.
64. Fuller, *Gospel Its Own Witness*, in *WAF*, 2:74–75.
65. Augustine, *City of God: Books 1–10*, IX.16, 297.
66. Fuller, *Gospel Its Own Witness*, in *WAF*, 2:82.

and "a determination to forsake every evil way."[67] Repentance from sin and reliance on Christ's moral atonement thus restored guilty criminals to the love of God and the imitation of his good character.

"The Grand Lesson which They Teach is Love": The Moral Wisdom of the Scriptures

Fuller defended the verity of Scripture against Paine and other Enlightenment thinkers influenced by Deism because he believed that its salutary precepts and instructions were vital for understanding and practicing true virtue.[68] Paine regarded the Scriptures as historically false, contradictory, fraught with immoral principles, and inherently discriminatory since all of humanity did not have equal access to them. He argued that nature was sufficient to teach rational humanity morality, equity, and freedom. Fuller countered that while nature had the capacity to reveal humanity's injustices and rebellion, it could not "recover them from it."[69] Humanity needed divine revelation to correct its depraved notions of good and evil and lead it in moral wisdom.

Hence, Fuller argued for the veracity of Scripture on the basis of its intrinsic goodness. He wrote, "it is not on the natural, but the moral, or rather the holy beauties of Scripture that I would lay the principal stress."[70] Since Scripture originated from God, its design, intentions, and expressions were not only factual but also good.

> A divinely-inspired production will not only be free from such blemishes as arise from vanity, and other evil dispositions of the mind, but will abound in those beauties which never fail to attend the genuine exercises of modesty, sensibility, and godly simplicity.[71]

Scripture was uncorrupted from human error and selfish interest. Therefore, it alone could serve as humanity's pure and righteous mentor in moral reformation.

---

67. Fuller, *Calvinistic and Socinian Systems Examined*, in WAF, 2:116.
68. Quote from Fuller, *Gospel Its Own Witness*, in WAF, 2:12.
69. Ibid., 2:19.
70. Ibid., 2:68.
71. Ibid., 2:64.

The Love of God Holds Creation Together

The main aretegenic import of the Scriptures rested in their instruction to love and worship God supremely. "The grand lesson which they teach is love; and love to God delights to express itself in acts of obedience, adoration, supplication, and praise."[72] God's Word not only guided readers in how to love God but it also motivated obedience and devotion. "The Scriptures . . . both inculcate and inspire the worship of God."[73] A love for God was inextricably tied to a love for his Word. "The words of Scripture are spirit and life. They are the language of love. Every exhortation of Christ and his apostles is impregnated with this spirit."[74] Love was the very essence of Scripture's communication. Thus, without a love for Scripture, one had no life in God and no love for virtue. Fuller stressed that the desire to love and worship God and cherish virtue was not natural to human beings—creatures needed the instruction and guidance that Scripture alone provided. The Bible unfolded the good character of God by highlighting his moral attributes and recording his righteous acts. It made humanity aware of the moral law to love God and their neighbor. By discovering God in the Scriptures and contemplating its exhortations to imitate him, readers learned love and moral excellence.

Scripture also uniquely exposed the wickedness of the human heart. Fuller likened it to a "mirror" that unveiled the inward person of "individual characters" as well as "the state of things as they move on in the great world."[75] As Fuller elaborated,

> Far from flattering the vices of mankind, it charges, without ceremony, every son of Adam with possessing the heart of an apostate. This charge it brings home to the conscience, not only by its pure precepts, and awful threatenings, but oftentimes by the very invitations and promises of mercy, which, while they cheer the heart with lively hope, carry conviction by their import to the very soul. In reading other books you may admire the ingenuity of the writer; but here your attention is turned inward. Read it but seriously, and your heart will answer to its descriptions.[76]

---

72. Ibid., 2:12.
73. Ibid., 2:11.
74. Ibid., 2:21.
75. Ibid., 2:64.
76. Ibid., 2:63.

"A System of Holiness": Fuller's Theology of Virtue

Most literature, Fuller perceived, gratified humanity's lust, pride, arrogance, and vanity. In contrast, the Scriptures summoned its readers to forsake those inclinations and find happiness in knowing God.

In contrast to all human creations, the divinely-inspired Scriptures had the power to speak to the heart and transform the inward person.

> It is a distinguishing property of the Bible, that all its precepts aim directly at the heart. It never goes about to form the mere exterior of man. To merely external duties it is a stranger. It forms the lives of men no otherwise than by forming their dispositions. It never addresses itself to their vanity, selfishness, or any other corrupt propensity. You are not pressed to consider what men will think of you, or how it will affect your temporal interest; but what is right, and what is necessary to your eternal well-being.[77]

Many Enlightenment thinkers promoted social progress and advancement in morality through the medium of education, but Fuller—who was no enemy to education—judged its usefulness for morality limited and temporary at best. In contrast, Scripture "will bring conviction to your bosom."[78] It penetrated the reader's deepest passions, seeking to refine the moral conduct of men and women by enabling their hearts and minds to love God's moral purity.

Fuller questioned the utility of philosophy to profit the morals of men and women. "Philosophy is little in comparison with Christianity." A philosophical system that attempted to ascertain truth and ethics without God had no hope of leading men and women to the source of goodness. "Philosophy may expand our ideas of creation," but "it neither inspires a love to the moral character of the Creator, nor a well-grounded hope of eternal life." In contrast, divine revelation offered "the only medium" to know and love virtue; it positioned readers "on nature's Alps," where "we discover things which eye hath not seen, nor ear heard, and of which it never hath entered the heart of man to conceive."[79]

---

77. Ibid., 2:15.
78. Ibid., 2:64.
79. Ibid., 2:97.

Conclusion

Fuller judged that the aretegenic value of the gospel lay in its invitation to rely solely on God for virtue. The character of God provided the source and standard of goodness, and thus knowing and loving him was the vehicle to knowing and loving virtue. In loving God supremely rather than the self, men and women learned to love their neighbor and treat others with dignity—fulfilling the moral law. A Calvinist understanding of human nature was salutary even though it could appear quite negative. It humbled men and women to admit their moral inability to achieve virtue, calling them to forsake their evil and turn to righteousness. The moral atonement of Christ furnished humanity with hope for pardon for its sins. It maintained moral order and displayed to creation God's justice and his merciful love for criminals. Christ's divine nature was essential to the success of the atonement—it made him distinctly qualified to satisfy God's justice and draw creation's attention to the gravity of God's willingness to love sinners. The moral law entailed a love of Christ for all of his divine natural and moral perfections—virtue was impossible without it. Faith in Christ's deity and moral atonement was vital to entering into a life of knowing, loving, and imitating God. Humanity's conflicting moral inclinations necessitated reliance on divine instruction to know true virtue. Scripture not only taught humanity about God's character and the gospel but it also held power to pierce and mold the hearts of men and women. Scripture produced moral fruits in the lives of its adherents, testifying to its goodness and veracity.

Fuller challenged the proponents of the new moral philosophy that it was deeply unwise to exclude God from morality. Every doctrine of the gospel proved salutary to the lives of believers, rousing a love for God that pervaded the agent's entire being.

> It might fairly be argued, in favour of the tendency of Calvinistic doctrines to promote the love of God, that, upon those principles, we have more to love him for than upon the other. On this system, we have much to be forgiven; and, therefore, love much. The expense at which our salvation has been obtained, as we believe, furnishes us with a motive of love to which nothing can be compared.[80]

---

80. Fuller, *Calvinistic and Socinian Systems Examined*, in WAF, 2:116.

5

"Abide in the Vine": The Source and Motivation of Virtue

IN RESPONSE TO THE proponents of the new moral philosophy of his day, Andrew Fuller maintained that Evangelical Calvinist beliefs about God's moral glory, human depravity, Christ's deity and moral atonement, and the authority of Scripture alone offered hope for true virtue.[1] The gospel summoned moral agents to forsake evil, secure righteousness through faith in Christ, and transform their passions and conduct through advancing their knowledge and love of God. In resting his apology on moral grounds, Fuller strove to not only defend Christian belief but also to preserve a notion of truth that was waning even in Christian theology. As Ellen Charry has written,

> The secularization, elevation, and constriction of reason in the seventeenth and eighteenth centuries undercut the sapiential, aretegenic, and participatory dimensions of doctrinal interpretations. Although Protestant scholastics like John Gerhard insisted on the sapiential function of theology, the dominant goal became laying out the pattern of Christian doctrines so that Christians would assent to correct propositions. Now the church had always insisted on right belief, but . . . it was right belief in the service of devotion.[2]

---

1. The quote in the chapter title is from Fuller, *Calvinistic and Socinian Systems Examined*, in *WAF*, 2:173.
2. Charry, *Renewing of Your Minds*, 237.

Fuller held that the import of orthodox theology lay in its salutary power to motivate and instill virtue in the lives of believers. Growth in the knowledge and love of Christian truth went hand in hand with growing in moral excellence, love for God and neighbor, and genuine happiness.

"Truth Ought to Be Dearer to Us": Knowing and Loving Christian Doctrine

According to Fuller, the aretegenic value of Christian truth had no power unless the believer had both knowledge and love for it.[3] Knowledge of the truth devoid of love offered no advantage to the believer's morality or happiness. Likewise, love that lacked knowledge of divine truth failed to conform men and women to the standard of virtue. Without the knowledge of God, human beings devoted their love to idols and the self and ultimately succumbed to corrupt and evil masters. Fuller's stress on rightly understanding the relationship between knowing and loving the truth was rooted in his pastoral concern to advance the holiness, virtuous character, and devotional life of men and women. This theme appeared not only in Fuller's writings against the Socinians and Deists but it also permeated almost all of his theological controversies. Two further examples—namely Fuller's writings against Robert Robinson (1735–1790) and Sandemanianism—illustrate the central role that this framework played in his thinking.

In his first letter to Robinson, Fuller insisted that the "importance of truth is itself a truth." [4] When Robinson received criticism for abandoning orthodox views of the Trinity, he responded that what ultimately mattered was right morality rather than accurate belief. Fuller found Robinson's notion of truth defective, for it eliminated morality from right knowledge.

> You have observed, I dare say, that it is very common to represent truth, and the belief of it, as of small account, and morality as all in all; nay, more, that the preaching of the former is the way to subvert the latter. And yet how easy were it to prove that this is no other than destroying the means in order to effect the end! Whatever may be pretended, I believe it will be found that all sin springs from error, or the belief of some falsehood; and all holy actions

---

3. The quote in the subheading is from Fuller, *Gospel Worthy of All Acceptation*, in *WAF*, 2:397.

4. Fuller, *Strictures on Some of the Leading Sentiments of Mr. R. Robinson*, in *WAF*, 3:588. For more on Robinson, see chap. 3.

from the belief of the truth. The former appears in that the will of man is so constituted as never to choose any thing but an apparent good. It is impossible we should choose what appears to us at the same time and in the same respects unlovely. Therefore whenever we choose evil we must believe evil to be lovely; that is, we must believe a falsehood. This the Scripture represents as calling "evil good, and good evil." And thus all vice springs from error, or false views of things.[5]

Right knowledge provided the vehicle for fruitful morality. A rejection of the truth of the gospel indicated as much about the agent's heart as it did the mind. Those who disbelieved the gospel had no love for the moral character of God, concern for the dignity and welfare of their neighbor, distaste for sin, or affection for the Savior. Fuller held that there was no morality "in the world" but "what arises from a conviction of the truth."[6] He believed that the proclamation of the gospel offered the ultimate means to promote goodness and happiness throughout the world: the "truth wants to be universally realized in order to produce universal holiness."[7]

Fuller most explicitly articulated his understanding of how both knowing and loving the truth were essential to true faith and moral development in his writings against the Sandemanians.[8] He found the Sandemanian movement so ruinous to morality that he addressed the matter in an appendix to the second edition of *The Gospel Worthy of All Acceptation* (1801) and in a later work entitled *Strictures on Sandemanianism* (1810). The Sandemanians rested faith exclusively in the agent's intellectual faculty, claiming that its essence consisted solely in a "general assent to the doctrines of revelation." Fuller granted that the Sandemanians espoused the right propositions, but their belief was "unaccompanied with love to them."[9] Fuller objected that a love for truth was essential to genuine belief. Citing 2 Thess 2:10–12, Fuller wrote, "faith is here called a receiving the love of the truth . . . that they might be saved."[10] For Fuller, belief in the gospel inescapably involved loving and conforming to its precepts. The Christian

5. Ibid., 3:590.
6. Ibid., 3:590–91.
7. Ibid., 3:591.
8. For more on Fuller's engagement with the Sandemanians, see Haykin, "Andrew Fuller and the Sandemanian Controversy," 223–36; and Finn's "Editor's Introduction" to Fuller, *Apologetic Works 5*, XV-32.
9. Fuller, *Gospel Worthy of All Acceptation*, in WAF, 2:329.
10. Ibid., 2:360.

faith was useless if reduced to a factual system devoid of any moral and sapiential worth.

Fuller affirmed that true understanding necessitated "spiritual knowledge."[11] Spiritual knowledge summoned men and women to experience and savor the goodness of truth with the purpose of conforming one's character and passions to Christ. Fuller elucidated what spiritual knowledge entailed by quoting a lengthy passage from Jonathan Edwards's work *Religious Affections* (1746).[12]

> There is a distinction to be made between a mere notional understanding, wherein the mind only beholds things in the exercise of a speculative faculty; and the sense of the heart, wherein the mind does not only speculate and behold, but relishes and feels. . . . The one is mere speculative knowledge; the other sensible knowledge, in which more than the mere intellect is concerned; the heart is the proper subject of it, or the soul as a being that not only beholds, but has inclination, and is pleased or displeased. And yet there is the nature of instruction in it; as he that has perceived the sweet taste of honey knows much more about it than he who has only looked upon and felt of it.[13]

Throughout his career, Fuller labored to challenge the Socinians, Deists, Antinomians, Sandemanians, and anyone else reading his theology to know and enjoy the moral beauty of divine truth. He found his opponents' moral systems defective because their notions of knowledge were deficient. Thus, he challenged them to recognize the limits of a merely natural and notional knowledge to produce morality, inviting them to embrace a spiritual knowledge that awakened their "sense of the heart"[14] and enabled them to apprehend and partake of the goodness of the gospel.

For both Edwards and Fuller, the culmination of the spiritual sense lay in knowing the moral glory of God and experiencing the transforming power of the truths of the gospel.

> Spiritual understanding primarily consists in this sense, or taste, of the moral beauty of Divine things; so that no knowledge can be called spiritual any further than it arises from this, and has this in

---

11. Fuller, *Strictures on Sandemanianism*, in *WAF*, 2:602.

12. Ibid., 2:602–6. The quote spans six pages in the Yale edition of *Religious Affections*. Edwards, *Religious Affections*, in *WJE*, 2:270–75.

13. Quoted Fuller, *Strictures on Sandemanianism*, in *WAF*, 2:604.

14. Ibid.

it. But, secondarily, it includes all that discerning and knowledge of things of religion which depends upon and flows from such a sense. When the true beauty and amiableness of the holiness, or true moral good, that is in Divine things, is discovered to the soul, it as it were opens a new world to its view. This shows the glory of all the perfections of God, and of every thing appertaining to the Divine Being; for, as was observed before, the beauty of all arises from God's moral perfections. This shows the glory of all God's works, both of creation and providence; for it is the special glory of them that God's holiness, righteousness, faithfulness, and goodness are so manifested in them; and without these moral perfections there would be no glory in that power and skill with which they are wrought. The glorifying of God's moral perfections is the special end of all the works of God's hands. By this sense of the moral beauty of Divine things is understood the sufficiency of Christ as a Mediator; for it is only by the discovery of the beauty of the moral perfections of Christ that the believer is let into the knowledge of the excellence of his person, so as to know any thing more of it than the devils do: and it is only by the knowledge of the excellence of Christ's person that any know his sufficiency as a Mediator; for the latter depends upon and arises from the former. It is by seeing the excellence of Christ's person that the saints are made sensible of the preciousness of his blood, and its sufficiency to atone for sin; for therein consists the preciousness of Christ's blood, that it is the blood of so excellent and amiable a person. And on this depends the meritoriousness of his obedience, and sufficiency and prevalence of his intercession. By this sight of the moral beauty of Divine things is seen the beauty of the way of salvation by Christ; for that consists in the beauty of the moral perfections of God, which wonderfully shines forth in every step of this method of salvation from beginning to end.... And, in the way's being contrived so as to attain these ends, consists the excellent wisdom of that way. By this is seen the excellence of the word of God: take away all the moral beauty and sweetness in the word, and the Bible is left wholly a dead letter, a dry, lifeless, tasteless thing.[15]

Edwards and Fuller exhorted readers to grow in wisdom and virtue by means of a spiritual knowledge of the moral glory of God, the person and atoning work of Christ, and the Word of God. Spiritual knowledge uniquely had the capacity to "bring us to the happiness which consists

---

15. Ibid., 2:605.

in the possession and enjoyment of moral good, in a way sweetly agreeing with God's moral perfections."[16] The moral law summoned men and women to know God spiritually by loving him with the heart, soul, mind, and strength. Such knowledge was the chief means for attaining lasting virtue and happiness.

Fuller anticipated two seemingly valid objections: if right belief facilitated virtue, why then do unbelievers not seem entirely bereft of virtue and happiness? Also, why do those who know the truth still experience moral failure and unhappiness? Fuller responded that the degree of a person's virtue and happiness corresponded with the degree of his or her knowledge and love of divine truth. "Whatever virtue there may be among Socinian converts," Fuller wrote, arose from the "principles which they hold in common with us, namely, the resurrection of the dead, and a future life."[17] Fuller attributed the source of morality for Paine and other Deists primarily in their affirmation of the "doctrine of a future life."[18] The belief instilled in them a general yet holy fear that their actions in this life mattered for the next. Right belief furnished Christians and non-Christians alike with the "springs of their virtue."[19] At the conclusion of his first letter to Robinson, Fuller wrote,

> Should it be asked, then why is not universal holiness found in good men who believe the truth? The answer is, though they believe the truth, they believe not the whole truth, nor perhaps do they wholly believe any truth. When they shall be perfectly delivered from "an evil heart of unbelief," they shall possess perfect holiness.[20]

According to Fuller, the key to growing in virtue was not to assume a posture of indifference to religious belief—as many of the leaders of

---

16. Ibid.

17. Fuller, *Calvinistic and Socinian Systems Examined*, in WAF, 2:136.

18. Fuller elaborated, "It is a fact that the passions of hope and fear are planted in our nature by Him who made us; and it may be presumed they are not planted there in vain.... Some are hereby taught the evil of their ways to a good purpose, and all are fairly warned, and their perseverance in sin is rendered inexcusable." Fuller suggested that God graciously created men and women with an innate fear of judgment to help restrain them from acting on their evil inclinations. Fuller, *Gospel Its Own Witness*, in WAF, 2:23, 26.

19. Fuller, *Calvinistic and Socinian Systems Examined*, in WAF, 2:136.

20. Fuller, *Strictures on Some of the Leading Sentiments of Mr. R. Robinson*, in WAF, 3:591. Fuller cited Heb 3:12.

Rational Dissent had suggested[21]—but rather to cherish and believe the truth more.

"A Portion Worthy to Be Sought": The Paradox of the Love of God

Fuller believed that the path to moral excellence and emotional fulfillment for humanity lay in a paradox: a disinterested love of God served the best interests of human beings.[22] The irony of prioritizing the love of God over love of self was that it more truly advanced the creature's welfare. The one who loves God as the Supreme Being "seeks his own well-being in connexion with the general good." When the agent put love of self first, his or her interests clashed with the general good. Fuller assigned an important place for love of self—in fact Scripture "requires us to love ourselves as we love our neighbor"—but elevated self-love terminated on the individual and detracted from the welfare of the whole.[23] The love of God and his moral goodness, however, profited not only one's neighbor and the general good but also the self. No agent existed above or untouched by the created order, and thus the good of the whole was beneficial to the welfare of the individual.

Fuller stressed that men and women must love God disinterestedly, or unselfishly. For Fuller, disinterested love entailed affection and adoration for God himself.

> And as to the enjoyment of the Divine favour, a proper pursuit of this object, instead of being at variance with disinterested affection, clearly implies it; for no man can truly desire the favour of God as his chief good, without a proportionate esteem of his character, and that for its own excellency. It is impossible that the favour of any being whose character we disapprove should be sought as our chief good, in preference to every other object in the universe. But a cordial approbation of the Divine character is the same thing as a disinterested affection to virtue.[24]

21. Priestley submitted that an "indifference to religion in general" was "favourable to the distinguishing between truth and falsehood." Quoted Fuller, *Calvinistic and Socinian Systems Examined*, in *WAF*, 2:135.

22. The quote in the subheading is from Fuller, *Remarks on Mr. Martin's Publication*, in *WAF*, 2:726.

23. Fuller, *Gospel Its Own Witness*, in *WAF*, 2:24.

24. Ibid., 2:25.

The Love of God Holds Creation Together

An agent's love for God must exist as an end in itself independent "from every selfish consideration."[25] Creation's ultimate end consisted in knowing and loving God. Thus, disinterested love required creatures to not elevate any motive or end above the love of God for its own sake. Only when creatures learned to relish the excellence of God's moral character for who he is can they begin to love the essence of virtue for what it is. When men and women enjoy God himself, they discover the enjoyment of virtue itself.

Loving God as an end in itself held enormous benefit for the creature, Fuller maintained. In emphasizing disinterested love, Fuller clarified that he had no intention to "separate the glory of God and our best interests, and to make it incumbent on men to pursue the one so as to neglect the other." Nor did disinterested love of God's character imply "loving him for some abstract principles of his nature" that in "no way related to his creatures."[26] Rather, disinterested love for God liberated men and women from their selfish love and the conflict it created with their neighbors. It enabled them to experience genuine, unpolluted love that united them with God and their neighbors in justice and charity. As Fuller explained,

> When I speak of loving God for himself, I neither suppose it is on account of some excellences in his nature which have no relation to our welfare, nor that we feel, regardless of our best interests, true honour, or substantial happiness. These may, and ought, no doubt, to be pursued in subordination to God's glory; and a proper pursuit of them, instead of setting aside the idea of love to God for his own excellence, necessarily implies it. . . . I must necessarily love him for what he is in himself. . . . Am I in pursuit of substantial happiness? If I am, I am in search of the enjoyment of God, as my everlasting portion; but how could I conceive of God as a portion worthy to be sought, or at all adapted to make me happy, unless I loved him for what he is in himself antecedently to my enjoyment of him? Do men ever seek a portion in earthly things without viewing that portion as good and desirable in itself, whether they have it or not?[27]

When creatures made the love of God their ultimate end, all other pure and righteous ends fell into place.[28]

25. Ibid.
26. Fuller, *Remarks on Mr. Martin's Publication*, in WAF, 2:726.
27. Ibid., 2:727.
28. Fuller's stress on loving the supreme good for its own sake as a means for happiness paralleled Augustine's assertion that "if we desire" the supreme good "not for the

Belief in the gospel supplied the chief means of producing disinterested love for God in moral agents. Only "faith in Christ" served as a successful "method" to secure the "exercise of disinterested and enlarged virtue." Belief in the gospel called the agent to "cordially acquiesce" in the "holy government of God" and in Christ's "mediation," inculcating affection for his character and a desire to attribute all moral glory to him. It invited sinners to renounce their selfish and criminal inclinations and it filled them with "devotedness to God and benevolence to men."[29] The doctrines of the gospel united men and women in "one heart with the Saviour," a bond that transformed believers into his righteousness and love. The path to disinterested love rested in the gospel, for it offered the single greatest display of God's moral character and grace. Therefore, any profession of love for God and virtue that had no basis in the gospel was in fact selfish love devoid of any profit to the creature and the general good.

Virtues of the Gospel

Christian truth—when approached with spiritual knowledge and disinterested love—motivated a life of virtuous behavior and happiness in men and women. The "best principles," Fuller affirmed, were those "which furnish the most effectual motives" for moral excellence.[30] Christianity's effectiveness to instill virtue in believers attested to the goodness and veracity of its precepts.

> Now there is not a doctrine in the whole compass of Christianity but what is improvable to this purpose. It is a grand peculiarity of the gospel that none of its principles are merely speculative; each is pregnant with a practical use.[31]

Christianity's success in motivating morality was based ultimately in its promotion of the love of God, love of Christ, and veneration for the Scriptures, which Fuller counted "cardinal virtues of the Christian character" in their

---

sake of anything else but for its own sake alone," it will "leave us nothing further to seek for our happiness. For this reason it is called the final good, since we want other things for the sake of it but want it only for its own sake." Augustine, *City of God: Books 1–10*, VIII.8, 251.

29. Fuller, *Gospel Its Own Witness*, in *WAF*, 2:25.
30. Ibid., 2:21.
31. Ibid., 2:22.

own right.[32] As the last chapter examined, Fuller believed that the Evangelical understanding of God's moral glory, Christ's moral atonement, and the Scripture's moral wisdom grounded true virtue. Thus, he included the love of these truths in the list of virtues that Christianity motivated. Since the test of a system's veracity lay in its design to promote moral goodness, Fuller devoted a significant proportion of his writings against the Socinians and Deists to showing the superiority of Christianity in motivating virtues such as benevolence, humility, charity, gratitude, and happiness.

Christianity nourished a benevolent spirit and demeanor in men and women. True benevolence arose from love for one's neighbor, which Fuller reiterated must first "consist with love to God."

> Whatever pretences may be made to devotion, or love to God, we never admit them to be real, unless accompanied with love to men; neither should any pretence of love to men be admitted as genuine, unless it be accompanied with love to God.[33]

The love of God and a heart of benevolence existed in harmony. Fuller warned against confusing benevolence with partiality, complacency, or esteem. He defined benevolence as "good-will to men," but "good-will to men is distinct from a good opinion of their principles or their practices." Benevolence did not exist without sincere candor. Treating one's neighbor with candor required a "temper of mind which will induce us to treat him openly, fairly, and ingenuously." A complacent disregard for the spiritual welfare of one's neighbor had nothing to do with true benevolence. Christians exercised benevolence most by communicating the gospel to others. "If religious principle of any kind should be found necessary to salvation, and if benevolence consist in that good-will to men," it followed that "the welfare of men is promoted by speaking the truth concerning them."[34] Fuller regarded "false principles" as "pernicious and destructive" to human beings—thus, benevolence was incomplete unless it extended to both body and soul.[35]

Alongside benevolence and love for neighbor, Christianity instilled the virtue of humility in believers. In contrast, the Enlightenment systems that advocated love of self as the medium of moral progress were prone to

---

32. Fuller, *Calvinistic and Socinian Systems Examined*, in *WAF*, 2:136.
33. Ibid., 2:162.
34. Ibid., 2:163.
35. Ibid., 2:164.

evoke the opposite of humility in men and women. Fuller distinguished between two forms of pride, natural and spiritual: "Both consist in a too high esteem of ourselves," one in natural accomplishments "which pertain to us as men," and the other in spiritual accomplishments, "which pertain to us as good men."[36] Fuller judged the Enlightenment presumptions of his age to be rooted in pride. Ascribing progress in knowledge chiefly to man's rational faculties sprang from natural pride, while resting moral progress in man's innate goodness manifested spiritual pride. Fuller employed the distinction between natural and moral inability to discern the true source of human virtue.

> It is true Dr. Priestley, and, for aught I know, all other writers, except atheists, acknowledge themselves indebted to God for the powers by which virtue is attained, and, perhaps, for the means of attaining it; but this is not acknowledging that we are indebted to him for virtue itself. Powers and opportunities are mere natural blessings; they have no virtue in them, but are a kind of talent, capable of being improved or not improved. Virtue consists not in the possession of natural powers, any more than in health, or learning, or riches; but in the use that is made of them. God does not, therefore, upon this principle, give us virtue. Dr. Priestley contends, that as we are "God's workmanship, and derive all our powers of body and mind from him, we cannot conceive of ourselves as being in a state of greater dependence upon him." The apostle Paul, however, teaches the necessity of being "created in Christ Jesus unto good works." According to Paul, we must become his workmanship by a new creation, in order to the performance of good works; but according to Dr. Priestley, the first creation is sufficient. . . .
>
> I do not deny that all men have natural powers, together with means and opportunities of doing good; which, if they were but completely well-disposed, are equal to the performance of their whole duty. God requires no more of us than to love and serve him with all our strength. These powers and opportunities render them accountable beings, and will leave them without excuse at the last day. But if they are not rightly disposed, all their natural powers will be abused; and the question is, to whom are we indebted for a change of disposition? If to God, we have reason to lie in the dust.[37]

---

36. Ibid., 2:170.
37. Ibid., 2:174.

The Love of God Holds Creation Together

Christianity inculcated the virtue of humility by teaching men and women to rely on God rather than the self for virtue. Although human nature possessed the natural powers for choosing virtue, the desires of the will militated against it. Men and women needed a new creation in Christ with new moral and spiritual capacities that enabled them to love and practice the good. Thus, creatures must ascribe any moral achievement to God—such was the pure and humbling nature of the gospel.

The aretegenic nature of the gospel diminished human pretension and directed men and women to rest their dignity in knowing God, and their goodness in trusting him. Christ and the apostles preached "human depravity, and salvation by free and sovereign grace through Jesus Christ" in order to "lay men low in the dust before God."[38] All of Christian doctrine, Fuller claimed, served to inspire humility in believers.

> Christ and his apostles inculcated humility, by teaching the primitive Christians that virtue itself was not of themselves, but the gift of God. They not only expressly declared this with respect to faith, but the same, in effect, of every particular included in the general notion of true godliness. "As the branch cannot bear fruit of itself," said Christ, "except it abide in the vine, no more can ye except ye abide in me:" for "without me ye can do nothing." . . . "He worketh in us both to will and to do, of his good pleasure." The manifest design of these important sayings was to humble the primitive Christians, and to make them feel their entire dependence upon God for virtue, even for every good thought.[39]

Belief in the gospel motivated humility by summoning believers to rely on God and give him glory rather than the creature.

Christianity also engendered the virtue of charity. By observing and loving God's good character, Christians learned to extend grace, sympathy, and kindness to their neighbor.

> Charity, it is allowed, will induce us to put the most favourable construction upon things, and to entertain the most favourable opinion of persons, that truth will admit. It is far from the spirit of Christianity to indulge a censorious temper, or to take pleasure in drawing unfavourable conclusions against any person whatever;

---

38. Ibid., 2:172.
39. Ibid., 2:173. Fuller cited John 15:4 and Phil 2:13.

but the tenderest disposition towards mankind cannot convert truth into falsehood, or falsehood into truth.⁴⁰

Fuller defended Christians against charges of bigotry for holding and promoting their convictions, explaining that they advocated them out of a concern for the welfare of humanity, not its detriment. For Fuller, nothing was more uncharitable than withholding the truth and glory of the gospel from others.

"Come Ye to the Waters": The Gospel a Source of Real Happiness

Fuller rested the source of real happiness in the knowledge and love of God. Loving God above all else served the best interests of the creature's enjoyment.

> Though the happiness of creatures be not admitted to be the final end of God's moral government, yet it is freely allowed to occupy an important place in the system. God is good, and his goodness appears in leaving so blended the honour of his name with the felicity of his creatures, that in seeking the one they should find the other. In so important a light do we consider human happiness, as to be willing to allow that to be the true religion which is most adapted to promote it.⁴¹

Fuller counted the conduciveness of a system to motivate happiness among the tests of its truthfulness. He resisted the trends of his age to depict Christianity as cheerless. "Our opponents" so commonly "represent the Calvinistic system as gloomy, as leading to melancholy and misery," for "our ideas of God, of sin, and of future punishment, they say, must necessarily depress our minds." He granted that Christianity had no design to bring joy to those who continued in unbelief. "While men are at war with God, we do not know of any evangelical promise that is calculated to make them happy."⁴² Christian doctrine undermined the empty delights that humanity desperately pursued to make them happy, replacing them with the pleasures that accompanied the love of God and life in Christ.

---

40. Ibid., 2:175.
41. Fuller, *Gospel Its Own Witness*, in *WAF*, 2:49. The quote in the subheading is from ibid., 2:52. Fuller cited Isa 55:1.
42. Fuller, *Calvinistic and Socinian Systems Examined*, in *WAF*, 2:206.

Fuller labored to expose false notions of happiness in order to elucidate its true nature. "Our system," he made clear, "is not adapted to promote that kind of cheerfulness and happiness to which men in general are greatly addicted."[43] Fuller explained,

> There is a kind of cheerfulness which resembles that of a tradesman who avoids looking into his accounts, lest they should disturb his peace and render him unhappy. This, indeed, is the cheerfulness of a great part of mankind, who shun the light, lest it should disturb their repose, and interrupt their present pursuits. They try to persuade themselves that they shall have peace, though they add drunkenness to thirst; and there are not wanting preachers who afford them assistance in the dangerous delusion. . . . Instead of considering mankind as lost sinners, exposed to everlasting destruction, they love to represent them simply as creatures, as the children of God, and to suppose that, having, in general, more virtue than vice, they have nothing to fear . . . have no reason to be afraid of endless punishment. These things, to be sure, make people cheerful; but it is with the cheerfulness of a wicked man.[44]

For Fuller, men and women who rejected the truth of the gospel could have nothing deeper than superficial and delusional happiness. The happiness of the unbeliever had "no virtue in it," Fuller claimed. Humanity based its contentment in "self-deceit and levity of spirit" rather than righteousness and the knowledge of God. Such happiness "may blaze awhile in the bosoms of the dissipated and the secure," but its vitality "will expire" when the finite objects of human desire fail.[45] Fuller listed the anchors that men and women throughout history have often tended to tie the security of their happiness to: an increase of knowledge, scientific refinement, political revolutions, improved systems of morality, and the final extinction of wars. None of these things were morally corrupt per se, but unlike the love of God such "public principles" had no power to endure.[46]

In contrast, Fuller attributed genuine happiness, peace, and cheerfulness to Christian faith and love for evangelical truths.

> Those who adopt the Calvinistic doctrine of the exceeding sinfulness of sin, and of their own lost condition as sinners, are prepared

---

43. Ibid., 2:207.
44. Ibid.
45. Ibid.
46. Fuller, *Gospel Its Own Witness*, in WAF, 2:55.

> to imbibe the joy of the gospel, supposing it to exhibit a great salvation, through the atonement of a great Saviour, to which others of opposite sentiments must of necessity be strangers.[47]

Christians reaped a "joy and peace in believing," realizing true comfort in discovering that their sins were forgiven and they no longer faced God's judgment.[48] By knowing and loving God, they participated in his divine happiness in righteousness and holiness. Through Christian worship, the glory of God filled believers' hearts with admiration and wonder.

According to Fuller, "no definition of happiness can be complete which includes not peace of mind, which admits not of perpetuity, or which meets not the necessities and miseries of human life." He believed that Christianity alone met these three criteria. First, Christianity promoted peace with God and neighbor, while other systems based on the love of self caused strife. Second, the happiness that the love of an infinitely good God engendered endured forever. In contrast, the "charms of youth and beauty quickly fade," and the "power of relishing natural enjoyments is soon gone." Natural pleasures do not flourish in old age, and "in death they are exterminated."[49] In contrast, Christian joys ripen with age and never perish. "To them the soil of age is friendly. . . . Who else can view death, judgment, and eternity with desire?"[50] Third, Christianity had a unique capacity to ameliorate the suffering of men and women and satisfy their yearning.

> It is depravity that directs us to seek satisfaction in something short of God; but it is owing to the nature of the soul that we are never able to find it. It is not possible that a being created immortal, and with a mind capable of continual enlargement, should obtain satisfaction in a limited good. Men may spend their time and strength, and even sacrifice their souls, in striving to grasp it, but it will elude their pursuit. It is only from an uncreated source that the mind can drink its fill. Here it is that the gospel meets our necessities. Its language is, "Ho, every one that thirsteth, come ye to the waters." . . . Jesus stood and cried, saying, "If any man thirst, let him come unto me, and drink."[51]

---

47. Fuller, *Calvinistic and Socinian Systems Examined*, in *WAF*, 2:210.
48. Ibid.
49. Fuller, *Gospel Its Own Witness*, in *WAF*, 2:50.
50. Ibid., 2:51.
51. Ibid., 2:52. Fuller cited Isa 55:1 and John 7:37.

Other securities provided temporary relief and shallow fulfillment at best, but the gospel promised lasting joy and peace.

"Those who enter most deeply into our views of things," Fuller maintained, "are among the happiest people in the world."[52] By plunging deeply into the love and knowledge of God, a believer drew from an eternal reservoir of peace and happiness. Knowing the grace and beauty of the gospel furnished forgiven sinners with ample motives for joy.

> It is affecting to think that man, originally pure, should have fallen from the height of righteousness and honour to the depth of apostacy and infamy—that he is now an enemy to God, and actually lies under his awful and just displeasure, exposed to everlasting misery—that, notwithstanding all this, a ransom is found to deliver him from going down to the pit—that God so loved the world as to give his only-begotten Son to become a sacrifice for sin, that whosoever believeth in him should not perish, but have eternal life . . . that the Holy Spirit is given to renew and sanctify a people for himself—that they who were under condemnation and wrath, being justified by faith in the righteousness of Jesus, have peace with God—that aliens and outcasts are become the sons and daughters of the Lord God Almighty—that everlasting arms are now beneath them, and everlasting glory is before them. These sentiments, I say, supposing them to be true, are undoubtedly affecting.[53]

"For the Healing of the Nations": Christianity's Moral Impact on Society

Fuller argued that Christianity benefited the moral conditions of society. In fact, he believed that where Christianity was absent, so was morality. "So much of the love of God and man as prevails in a nation, so much morality is there in it, and no more."[54] The knowledge and imitation of God stirred believers to practice righteousness, equity, and charity in their communities, promoting its welfare and peace. Fuller clarified that he did not include counterfeit forms of Christianity in this claim. "The Christianity here defended is not Christianity as it is corrupted by popish superstition"

---

52. Fuller, *Calvinistic and Socinian Systems Examined*, in *WAF*, 2:214.

53. Ibid., 2:209–10.

54. Fuller, *Gospel Its Own Witness*, in *WAF*, 2:39. The quote in the subheading is from ibid., 2:49

or "as interwoven with national establishments . . . for the purpose of promoting their political designs."⁵⁵ When human beings sever Christianity from Scripture, they shape it according to their evil inclinations and exploit the name to serve their selfish ends. Fuller granted that sincere believers often failed to love God and their neighbor perfectly. However, the good that Christians have produced far outweighed the bad.

Fuller called into question the common Enlightenment notion advocated by Paine that the ancient civilizations of Greece and Rome upheld true morality and reason until the Jews and Christians reversed and quashed it. "I am aware," Fuller wrote, "that deistical writers have laboured to hold up the modern as well as the ancient heathens in a very favourable light," applauding "their simplicity and virtue."⁵⁶ Fuller found no warrant in history for their high estimation of the morality of these cultures.

> Husbands also were allowed to impart the use of their wives to handsome and deserving men, in order to the producing of healthy and vigorous children for the commonwealth. . . . Children which were deformed, or of a bad constitution, were murdered. . . . This practice, with that of procuring abortion, was encouraged by Plato and Aristotle. . . . The unnatural love of boys was so common in Greece that in many places it was sanctioned by the public laws. . . . The Romans were allowed by Romulus to destroy all their female children except the eldest. . . . Gladiators shone, in which a number of slaves were engaged to fight for the diversion of the multitude till each one slew or was slain by his antagonist, were common among them. Of these brutish exercises the people were extremely fond; even the women ran eagerly after them, taking pleasure in seeing the combatants kill one another, desirous only that they should fall genteelly, or in an agreeable attitude! . . . Human sacrifices were offered up in almost all heathen countries. Children were burnt alive by their parents, to Baal, Moloch, and other deities.⁵⁷

Many of Fuller's contemporaries had opposed Christian missions on the basis that the heathen possessed just as much if not more morality than Christians. Fuller countered that "natural theology" did not suffice to

---

55. Ibid., 2:7.
56. Ibid., 2:42.
57. Ibid., 2:40–41.

make men and women good—they needed the revelation of Scripture and the gospel.[58]

Many submitted that the Chinese had superior morality than the Christian missionaries in China. Fuller objected that while the Chinese had a reputation for well-mannered outward behavior, many nonetheless degraded the humanity and dignity of women. "Many of the rich, as well as the poor, when they are delivered of daughters, stifle and kill them."[59] Fuller recognized that the moral conditions of countries in which Christianity had a presence still fell far short of perfection. Nonetheless, he maintained that these places would have been worse off without Christianity.

> Whatever we are, and whatever we may be, gross idolatry, I presume, may be considered as banished from Europe; and, thanks be to God, a number of its attendant abominations, with various other immoral customs of the heathen, are, in a good measure, banished with it. We have no human sacrifices; no gladiatory combats; no public indecencies between the sexes; no law that requires prostitution; no plurality or community of wives; no dissolving of marriages on trifling occasions; nor any legal murdering of children, or of the aged and infirm. If unnatural crimes be committed among us, they are not common; much less are they tolerated by the laws, or countenanced by public opinion. On the contrary, the odium which follows such practices is sufficient to stamp with perpetual infamy the first character in the land. Rapes, incests, and adulteries are not only punishable by law, but odious in the estimation of the public. It is with us, at least in a considerable degree, as it was in Judea, where he that was guilty of such vices was considered as a fool in Israel. The same, in less degrees, may be said of fornication, drunkenness, lying, theft, fraud, and cruelty: no one can live in the known practice of these vices, and retain his character.[60]

Fuller considered Christianity a major asset in shaping the general ethos, conscience, and ethical foundations of a society and in "meliorating the state of mankind."[61]

Fuller found the moral law to love God and one's neighbor as having considerable and immediate relevance to the social issues of his day. He did

---

58. Fuller, *Gospel Its Own Witness*, in *WAF*, 2:43.
59. Ibid.
60. Ibid., 2:42–43.
61. Ibid., 2:39.

not hesitate to indict his fellow Englishmen for the ways they failed to fulfill the moral law, especially for their participation and complicity in the slave trade. However, because human beings rarely promoted immorality so flagrantly and undisguised, the resistance of moral evil in society required spiritual wisdom grounded in the knowledge of God.

> Theft, cruelty, and murder . . . assume the names of wisdom and good policy ere a plea can be set up in their defense. Thus were the arguments for the abolition of the slave trade answered, and in this manner was that iniquitous traffic defended in the British parliament. Doubtless there is a woe hanging over the heads of those men who thus called evil good, and good evil.[62]

For Fuller, the evil of the slave trade in Britain paired with the violence incited by the French Revolution demonstrated that non-Christian systems furnished no motive to love one's neighbor. He attributed the efforts of Evangelical forces—led by his friend William Wilberforce—to abolish slavery to their Christian virtues of love and benevolence.

Conclusion

Fuller believed that spiritual knowledge and a disinterested love for God motivated virtuous behavior, thus testifying to Christianity's inherent goodness and truthfulness. Men and women learned virtue and had hope for real happiness by devoting their ultimate love to God and participating in his grace, goodness, and love. Following Christianity in a right manner yielded positive effects in believers' lives and even in society. The gospel liberated men and women from the miseries and evils wrought by self-love and rebellion to the Creator, giving them peace with God and with their neighbor. Thus, Fuller concluded, "Christianity is a living principle of virtue in good men," and "it affords this further blessing to society, that it restrains the vices of the bad. It is a tree of life whose fruit is immortality," and "whose very leaves are for the healing of the nations."[63]

---

62. Ibid., 2:8.
63. Ibid., 2:49.

6

Conclusion

ANDREW FULLER AIMED TO shake the foundations of British Enlightenment ethical thought by grounding true virtue in the doctrines of Evangelical Calvinism. He resisted the notion advanced by thinkers like Thomas Paine and Joseph Priestley that moral progress necessitated the abandonment of Christian orthodoxy. They replaced God with the self as normative for morality—human nature on its own had only to realize its ethical potential through education and freedom from oppressive social and religious structures. Reason rather than God became the universalizing moral principle that gave every agent equal advantage to knowing truth and virtue. For Paine and Priestley, God's role in human virtue was finished long ago when he created human nature with all the rational and moral faculties required to attain goodness and happiness. Fuller objected that the self was a precarious basis for morality and that men and women had no source for virtue without the Christian God.

Early in Fuller's ministry career, after personally wrestling through questions concerning moral accountability in his Particular Baptist church context, he became convinced that human beings had no excuse for their immorality and their rejection of the gospel. Unbelief was not due to any natural inability but to moral inability, leaving moral agents accountable for not loving and desiring good. All of humanity possessed equal natural ability to ascertain truth and justice, but its evil inclinations unfailingly opposed them. For Fuller, the very doctrines that Paine and Priestley derided as immoral provided humanity's only hope for renouncing evil and transforming hearts to embrace righteousness. This conviction motivated

Fuller's life mission to propagate the knowledge of God throughout the world by proclaiming the gospel.

Fuller based his response to Priestley and Paine on moral grounds because he understood the nature of truth to consist in both factuality and salutarity. As Ellen Charry demonstrated in her work, *By The Renewing of Your Minds*, the classic theologians defended orthodoxy against its challengers because they held that right knowledge and devotion to God provided the key means for engendering moral excellence and happiness in men and women. As Charry explained, modernist epistemology largely eliminated the moral dimension from truth, sacrificing *sapientia* for *scientia*. Fuller resisted such a shift, writing his tracts against Socinianism and Deism with the same pastoral motivation and understanding of truth as the classic theologians who preceded him. Fuller's views on moral inability clashed with the modernist reliance on human rational faculties to advance truth and morality in the world. Hence, Fuller rested virtue not in the self but in the moral character of God. In terms of the proportion of existence, God as the Supreme Being occupied the greatest and best position in the universe, comprehending all beauty, excellence, and goodness. The moral law represented the extension of his moral character, summoning men and women to love God and one's neighbor. Only by loving God could human beings love virtue and promote the welfare of others. The study of God taught men virtue, facilitating the imitation of his ways. The love and knowledge of God furnished humanity with the true universal principle of peace, benevolence, and equity.

For Fuller, a system of truth must correspond with moral order. Thus, he derived his understanding of virtue directly from his Evangelical Calvinism. His theology of virtue commenced with the moral character of God, which provided the source and standard of goodness. The ultimate and unifying end of creation lay in glorifying God by devoting its worship, obedience, and love to him. However, by subverting its *raison d'être* and relapsing to love of self, humanity became enslaved to its immoral passions and subjected itself to the righteous judgment of the Moral Governor. In order to satisfy his moral justice and yet extend love and mercy to sinners, God gave his righteous Son as an atonement. By renouncing their evil and resting faith in Christ's moral atonement, men and women found restoration in the love of God and thus true hope for righteousness. Through the influence of the Spirit, believers learned to look to God's Word for instruction in moral wisdom rather than their corrupt inclinations. Fuller assigned significant aretegenic import to these evangelical doctrines because they each summoned moral agents to rely on God entirely for virtue.

Right belief could not benefit a person unless he or she had both spiritual knowledge and disinterested love for God. Since Christian truth was comprised of more than mere information, in order to know it the agent must savor its goodness and beauty and participate in its transforming power. Love for God out of a genuine affection for who he is in himself must precede any other motive—otherwise the motive for the agent's love would be mixed with selfishness and self-love. However, the paradox of prioritizing the love of God for himself before self-love lay in the fact that it served the best interests of the agent. When creatures made the love of God their ultimate end, every other pure end and motive fell into its proper place. The love of God motivated men and women to grow in virtuous thoughts and actions and it inspired real and lasting happiness in their lives. It also benefited society by inspiring believers to love their neighbor and seek the welfare of the whole. A spiritual knowledge and disinterested love of God's moral character and grace stirred the hearts of believers to devote themselves to virtue.

Recent studies in virtue ethics help elucidate the relevance of Fuller's theology of virtue for today. In his work, *After Virtue*, Alisdair MacIntyre maintains that Enlightenment moral theory has failed because its understanding of human nature is incompatible with the moral injunctions it inherited. Christianity's moral precepts were designed to restore fallen creatures to their ultimate moral end to obey and glorify God, but modernist thinkers "reject any teleological view of human nature, any view of man as having an essence which defines his true end." For MacIntyre, the point of ethics is to "enable man to pass from his present state to his true end," but Enlightenment moral theories eliminated "any notion of man-as-he-could-be-if-he-realized-his-*telos*."[1] MacIntyre concludes,

> Hence the eighteenth-century moral philosophers engaged in what was an inevitably unsuccessful project; for they did indeed attempt to find a rational basis for their beliefs in a particular understanding of human nature, while inheriting a set of moral injunctions on the one hand and a conception of human nature on the other which had been expressly designed to be discrepant with each other.[2]

---

1. MacIntyre, *After Virtue*, 54.
2. Ibid., 55.

The failure of the Enlightenment to provide a basis for morality resulted in what MacIntyre labels emotivism, a notion widely-held by many today that "all moral judgments are nothing but expressions of preference . . . attitude or feeling."[3] MacIntyre and other virtue theorists call for a restoration of understanding virtue as set of moral characteristics that lead human beings in realizing *eudaimonia* (happiness and prosperity) and their moral *telos*.

Fuller had perceived the incongruity of the modernist anthropology and its moral claims long ago, charging that its moral foundations were doomed to fail as long as they rested on individualist self-love and conflicting human feelings. Fuller's ethical thought bears similarities with some aspects of modern virtue theory by stressing that virtuous characteristics in persons must exist conceptually and ontologically prior to virtuous actions.[4] However, the foundation of Fuller's moral ontology went beyond the person to the character of God. The pursuit of virtue consisted in more than simply evaluating persons by right moral character traits—such as equity, courage, benevolence, etc. Rather, the goodness of men and women was measured by whether they loved God and fulfilled their ultimate *telos* by enjoying and glorifying him. Since God as the Supreme Being comprehended all goodness, beauty, and moral glory, the attainment of virtue rested in loving him chiefly. The goodness of God consisted in his perfect determination and love for righteousness, and he called his creatures to participate in this love by resting faith in the gospel.

Fuller's moral theory represents an unabashedly theological account of virtue. He grounded his engagement with the ethical issues and moral philosophies of his day in his Evangelical Calvinistic theology, arguing that the essence of truth, righteousness, and happiness consists in right beliefs and affections for God. His writings continue to provoke pertinent questions for men and women today: Are the most educated people and nations the most moral ones? Is our culture's preoccupation with individualism and self-help conducive or harmful to virtue? Is God relevant for virtue today? If Fuller were asked today how men and women can grow in virtue, I imagine that he would urge us to deepen our knowledge and love of God.

---

3. Ibid., 12.

4. For more on different types of modern virtue theories, see Zagzebski, *Virtues of the Mind*.

Bibliography

Adams, John. *Diary and Autobiography of John Adams*. Edited by L. H. Butterfield. 4 vols. Cambridge: Harvard University Press, 1961.
Aldridge, Owen. *Thomas Paine's American Ideology*. Newark: University of Delaware Press, 1984.
Ascol, Tom. "The Doctrines of Grace: A Critical Analysis of Federalism in the Theologies of John Gill and Andrew Fuller." PhD diss., Southwestern Baptist Theological Seminary, 1989.
Augustine, Saint. *The City of God: Books 1–10*. Vol. 6, *The Works of Saint Augustine: A Translation for the 21st Century*. Edited by Boniface Ramsey. Translated by William Babcock. New York: New City, 2012.
———. *The City of God: Books 11–22*. Vol. 7, *The Works of Saint Augustine: A Translation for the 21st Century*. Edited by Boniface Ramsey. Translated by William Babcock. New York: New City, 2013.
Bebbington, D. W. *Evangelicalism in Modern Britain*. New York: Routledge, 2002.
Bowers, J. D. *Joseph Priestley and English Unitarianism in America*. University Park, PA: Pennsylvania State University Press, 2009.
Box, Bart. "Atonement in the Thought of Andrew Fuller." PhD thesis, New Orleans Baptist Theological Seminary, 2009.
Brewster, Paul. *Andrew Fuller: Model Pastor-Theologian*. Nashville: B & H, 2010.
Brooke, John H. "Joining Natural Philosophy to Christianity: The Case of Joseph Priestley." In *Heterodoxy in Early Modern Science and Religion*, edited by John Brooke and Ian Maclean, 319–36. Oxford: Oxford University Press, 2006.
———. "'A Sower Went Forth': Joseph Priestley and the Ministry of Reform." In *Motion Toward Perfection: The Achievement of Joseph Priestley*, edited by A. Truman Schwartz and John G. McEvoy, 21–56. Boston: Skinner, 1990.
Burke, Edmund. *Reflections on the Revolution in France, and on the Proceedings in Certain Societies in London Relative to That Event*. Vol. 5, *The Works of the Right Honourable Edmund Burke*. London: F. and C. Rivington, 1823.
Calkin, Homer L. "Pamphlets and Public Opinion During the American Revolution." *Pennsylvania Magazine of History and Biography* 64 (1940) 38–40.
Charry, Ellen. *By the Renewing of Your Minds*. New York: Oxford University Press, 1997.

Bibliography

Chun, Chris. *The Legacy of Jonathan Edwards in the Theology of Andrew Fuller*. Studies in the History of Christian Traditions 162. Leiden: Brill, 2012.

———. "A Mainspring of Missionary Thought: Andrew Fuller on Natural and Moral Ability." *American Baptist Quarterly* 25 (Winter 2006) 335–55.

Claeys, Gregory. *Thomas Paine: Social and Political Thought*. Boston: Unwin Hyman, 1989.

Clipsham, E. F. "Andrew Fuller and Fullerism: A Study in Evangelical Calvinism." *The Baptist Quarterly* 20 (1963–64) 99–114.

Conway, Moncure Daniel. *The Life of Thomas Paine*. New York: G. P. Putnam's Sons, 1892.

Crisp, Oliver D. "The Moral Government of God: Jonathan Edwards and Joseph Bellamy on the Atonement." In *After Jonathan Edwards: The Courses of New England Theology*, edited by Oliver D. Crisp and Douglas A. Sweeney, 78–90. New York: Oxford University Press, 2012.

Daniel, Curt. "Andrew Fuller and Antinomianism." In *"At the Pure Fountain of Thy Word": Andrew Fuller As an Apologist*, edited by Michael A. G. Haykin, 74–82. Studies in Baptist History and Thought 6. Eugene, OR: Wipf & Stock, 2006.

Edwards, Jonathan. *Ethical Writings*. Vol. 8, *The Works of Jonathan Edwards*. Edited by Paul Ramsey. New Haven: Yale University Press, 1989.

———. *Freedom of the Will*. Vol. 1, *The Works of Jonathan Edwards*. Edited by Paul Ramsey. New Haven: Yale University Press, 1957.

———. *Original Sin*. Vol. 3, *The Works of Jonathan Edwards*. Edited by Clyde A. Holbrook. New Haven: Yale University Press, 1970.

———. *Religious Affections*. Vol. 2, *The Works of Jonathan Edwards*. Edited by John E. Smith. New Haven: Yale University Press, 1959.

Everts, W. W. "Andrew Fuller." *The Review and Expositor* 17 (1920) 408–30.

Fiering, Norman. *Jonathan Edwards's Moral Thought and Its British Context*. Chapel Hill: University of North Carolina Press, 1981.

———. *Moral Philosophy at Seventeenth-Century Harvard*. Chapel Hill: University of North Carolina Press, 1981.

Foner, Eric. *Tom Paine and Revolutionary America*. New York: Oxford University Press, 1976.

Foster, Frank Hugh. *A Genetic History of the New England Theology*. Chicago: University of Chicago Press, 1907.

Fruchtman, Jack. "Nature and Revolution in Paine's *Common Sense*." *The History of Political Thought* 10 (1989) 421–38.

———. *Thomas Paine: Apostle of Freedom*. New York: Four Walls Eight Windows, 1994.

Fuller, Andrew. *Apologetic Works 1*. Vol. 5, *The Complete Works of Andrew Fuller*. Edited by Robert William Oliver. Berlin: De Gruyter, 2016.

———. *Apologetic Works 5: Strictures on Sandemanianism*. Vol. 9, *The Complete Works of Andrew Fuller*. Edited by Nathan A. Finn. Berlin: De Gruyter, 2016.

———. *The Complete Works of the Rev. Andrew Fuller with a Memoir of His Life by Andrew Gunton Fuller*. Edited by Joseph Belcher. 3 vols. Philadelphia: American Baptist Publication Society, 1845. Reprint, Harrisonburg, VA: Sprinkle, 1988.

———. *The Diary of Andrew Fuller, 1780-1801*. Vol. 1, *The Complete Works of Andrew Fuller*. Edited by Michael D. McMullen and Timothy D. Whelan. Berlin: De Gruyter, 2016.

———. *Memoirs of the Rev. Samuel Pearce*. Vol. 4, *The Complete Works of Andrew Fuller*. Edited by Michael A. G. Haykin. Berlin: De Gruyter, 2017.

Bibliography

Fuller, A. G. *Men Worth Remembering: Andrew Fuller*. London: Hodder and Stoughton, 1882.

Gibbs, F. W. *Joseph Priestley: Adventurer in Science and Champion of Truth*. London: Nelson, 1965.

Harris, Ian. "Paine and Burke: God, Nature and Politics." In *Public and Private Doctrine: Essays in British History Presented to Maurice Cowling*, edited by M. Bentley, 34–62. Cambridge: Cambridge University Press, 1993.

Haykin, Michael A. G. "Andrew Fuller and the Sandemanian Controversy." In *"At the Pure Fountain of Thy Word": Andrew Fuller As an Apologist*, edited by Michael A. G. Haykin, 223–35. Studies in Baptist History and Thought 6. Eugene, OR: Wipf & Stock, 2006.

———. *The Armies of the Lamb: The Spirituality of Andrew Fuller*. Classics of Reformed Spiritually 3. Dundas, ON: Joshua, 2001.

———. "Great Admirers of the Transatlantic Divinity." In *After Jonathan Edwards: The Courses of New England Theology*, edited by Oliver D. Crisp and Douglas A. Sweeney, 197–207. New York: Oxford University Press, 2012.

———. *One Heart and One Soul: Jonathan Sutcliff of Olney, His Friends and His Time*. Durham, UK: Evangelical, 1994.

———. "'The Oracles of God': Andrew Fuller's Response to Deism." In *"At the Pure Fountain of Thy Word": Andrew Fuller As an Apologist*, edited by Michael A. G. Haykin, 122–38. Studies in Baptist History and Thought 6. Eugene, OR: Wipf & Stock, 2006.

———. "Particular Redemption in the Writings of Andrew Fuller." In *The Gospel in the World*, edited by D. W. Bebbington, 107–28. Studies in Baptist History and Thought 1. Carlisle, UK: Paternoster, 2002.

———. "A Socinian and Calvinist Compared: Joseph Priestley and Andrew Fuller on the Propriety of Prayer to Christ." *Nederlands Archief voor Kerkgeschiedenis/Dutch Review of Church History* 73 (1993) 178–98.

———, ed. *"At the Pure Fountain of Thy Word": Andrew Fuller As an Apologist*. Studies in Baptist History and Thought 6. Eugene, OR: Wipf & Stock, 2006.

———, ed. *The Life and Thought of John Gill (1697–1771): A Tercentennial Appreciation*. Leiden: E. J. Brill, 1997.

Hiebert, Erwin N. "The Integration of Revealed Religion and Scientific Materialism in the Thought of Joseph Priestley." In *Joseph Priestley: Scientist, Theologian and Metaphysician*, edited by Lester Kieft and Bennet R. Willeford, Jr., 27–61. Lewisburg, PA: Bucknell University Press, 1980.

Hoselton, Ryan P. "Andrew Fuller's Aretology." *The Southern Baptist Journal of Theology* 17 (Summer 2013) 83.

———. "'A System of Holiness': Andrew Fuller's Evangelical Calvinistic Theology of Virtue." *Puritan and Reformed Journal* 6 (2014) 123–45.

———. "Thomas Paine and Democratic Religion in America." *Studia Territorialia* XV.3–4 (2015) 11–26.

Ivimey, Joseph. *A History of the English Baptists*. 4 vols. London: Burditt, Buxton, Hamilton, Baynes, etc., 1811–1830.

Jimack, Peter. "The French Enlightenment II: Deism, Morality and Politics." In *British Philosophy and the Age of the Enlightenment*, edited by Stuart Brown, 251–73. New York: Routledge, 1996.

Keane, John. *Tom Paine: A Political Life*. Boston: Little, Brown, 1995.

Bibliography

Kentish, John. *The Moral Tendency of Christian Doctrine. A Discourse, Written With to Mr. A. Fuller's Examination of the Calvinistic and Socinian Systems, and Delivered at Exeter, July 6th, 1796. Before the Society of Unitarian Christians, Established in the West of England for Promoting Christian Knowledge and the Practice of Virtue by the Distribution of Books*. 2nd ed. London: J. Johnson, 1798.

———. *Strictures Upon the Reply of Mr. A. Fuller to Mr. Kentish's Discourse, Entitled "The Moral Tendency of the Genuine Christian Doctrine."* London: J. Johnson, 1798.

Kirby, H. "The Theology of Andrew Fuller in its Relation to Calvinism." PhD thesis, Edinburgh University, 1956.

Kuklick, Bruce, ed. *Thomas Paine*. Burlington, VT: Ashgate, 2006.

Locke, John. *An Essay Concerning Human Understanding*. Edited by Peter H. Nidditch. New York: Oxford University Press, 1979.

MacIntyre, Alisdair. *After Virtue*. 3rd ed. Notre Dame: University of Notre Dame Press, 2007.

———. *A Short History of Ethics*. 2nd ed. Notre Dame: University of Notre Dame Press, 1998.

Marsden, George. *Jonathan Edwards: A Life*. New Haven: Yale University Press, 2003.

Mauldin, A. Chadwick. *Fullerism as Opposed to Calvinism: A Historical and Theological Comparison of the Missiology of Andrew Fuller and John Calvin*. Eugene, OR: Wipf & Stock, 2011.

May, Henry. *The Enlightenment in America*. New York: Oxford University Press, 1976.

McEvoy, J. G., and J. E. McGuire. "God and Nature: Priestley's Way of Rational Dissent." *Historical Studies in the Physical Sciences* 6 (1975) 325–404.

McNaughton, David. "British Moralists of the Eighteenth Century: Shaftesbury, Butler and Price." In *British Philosophy and the Age of the Enlightenment*, edited by Stuart Brown, 203–27. New York: Routledge, 1996.

Mohler, R. Albert, ed. "The Life and Ministry of Andrew Fuller." Special Issue, *The Southern Baptist Journal of Theology* 17 (Spring 2013).

———, ed. "The Life and Ministry of Andrew Fuller, Pt. 2." Special Issue, *The Southern Baptist Journal of Theology* 17.2 (Summer 2013).

Morden, Peter J. "Andrew Fuller: A Biographical Sketch." In *"At the Pure Fountain of Thy Word": Andrew Fuller As an Apologist*, edited by Michael A. G. Haykin, 1–42. Studies in Baptist History and Thought 6. Eugene, OR: Wipf & Stock, 2006.

———. *The Life and Thought of Andrew Fuller (1754–1815)*. Studies in Evangelical History and Thought. Milton Keynes, UK: Paternoster, 2015.

———. *Offering Christ to the World: Andrew Fuller (1754–1815) and the Revival of Eighteenth Century Particular Baptist Life*. Studies in Baptist History and Thought 8. Carlisle, UK: Paternoster, 2003.

Morris, J. W. *Memoirs of the Life and Death of the Rev. Andrew Fuller*. London: Wightman and Cramp, 1826.

Nettles, Tom J. *By His Grace and For His Glory*. Grand Rapids, MI: Baker, 1986.

———. "Christianity Pure and Simple: Andrew Fuller's Contest with Socinianism." In *"At the Pure Fountain of Thy Word": Andrew Fuller As an Apologist*, edited by Michael A. G. Haykin, 139–69. Studies in Baptist History and Thought 6. Eugene, OR: Wipf & Stock, 2006.

Noll, Mark. *America's God: From Jonathan Edwards to Abraham Lincoln*. New York: Oxford University Press, 2002.

———. *The Rise of Evangelicalism*. Downers Grove, IL: InterVarsity, 2003.

Bibliography

Nuttall, Geoffrey F. "Northamptonshire and the Modern Question: A Turning-Point in Eighteenth-Century Dissent." *Journal of Theological Studies* 16 (1965) 101–23.

Oliver, Robert. "The Emergence of a Strict and Particular Baptist Community Among the English Calvinistic Baptists, 1770–1850." DPhil thesis, London Bible College, 1986.

Paine, Thomas. *The Age of Reason, Part I*. In *Thomas Paine: Political Writings*, edited by Bruce Kuklick, 265–319. Cambridge: Cambridge University Press, 2000.

———. "Examination of Prophecies." In vol. 4, *The Writings of Thomas Paine*, edited by M. D. Conway. New York: G. P. Putnam's Sons, 1894–96.

Piper, John. *Andrew Fuller: I Will Go Down if You Will Hold the Rope!* Minneapolis: Desiring God, 2012.

Powell, David. *Tom Paine: The Greatest Exile*. New York: St. Martin's, 1985.

Priest, Gerald L. "Andrew Fuller, Hyper-Calvinism, and the 'Modern Question.'" In *"At the Pure Fountain of Thy Word": Andrew Fuller As an Apologist*, edited by Michael A. G. Haykin, 43–73. Studies in Baptist History and Thought 6. Eugene, OR: Wipf & Stock, 2006.

Priestley, Joseph. *Defences of Unitarianism for the Years 1788 and 1789*. Vol. 18, *The Theological and Miscellaneous Works of Joseph Priestley*. Edited by J. T. Rutt. New York: Klaus Reprint Co., 1972 (1790).

———. *A General History of the Christian Church, From the Fall of the Western Empire*. Vol. 10, *The Theological and Miscellaneous Works of Joseph Priestley*. Edited by J. T. Rutt. New York: Klaus Reprint Co., 1972 (1803).

———. *A History of the Corruptions of Christianity*. Keene, NH: J. and W. Prentiss, 1838.

———. *The Importance and Extent of Free Inquiry in Matters of Religion*. London: J. Johnson, 1785.

———. *Memoirs of Joseph Priestley*. London: Allenson, 1904.

———. *The Proper Objects of Education in the Present State of the World*. Vol. 15, *The Theological and Miscellaneous Works of Joseph Priestley*. Edited by J. T. Rutt. New York: Klaus Reprint Co., 1972 (1791).

———. *The Theological and Miscellaneous Works of Joseph Priestley*. Edited by J. T. Rutt. 25 vols. New York: Klaus Reprint Co., 1972.

Prochaska, Franklyn K. "Thomas Paine's *The Age of Reason* Revisited." *Journal of the History of Ideas* 33 (1972) 561–76.

Rivers, Isabel. *Reason, Grace, and Sentiment: A Study of the Language of Religion and Ethics in England, 1660–1780*. Vol. 1, *Whichcote to Wesley*. Cambridge: Cambridge University Press, 1991.

Roberts, Phil. "Andrew Fuller." In *Theologians of the Baptist Tradition*, edited by Timothy George and David S. Dockery, 34–51. Nashville: Broadman & Holman, 2001.

Ryland, John, Jr. *The Work of Faith, the Labour of Love, and the Patience of Hope, Illustrated: In the Life and Death of the Rev. Andrew Fuller*. 2nd ed. London: Button & Son, 1818.

Schofield, Robert E. *The Enlightenment of Joseph Priestley: A Study of His Life and Work from 1733 to 1773*. University Park: Pennsylvania State University Press, 1997.

Sell, Alan P. F. "Andrew Fuller and the Socinians." *Enlightenment and Dissent* 19 (2000) 91–115.

———. "*The Gospel Its Own Witness*: Deism, Thomas Paine and Andrew Fuller." In *Enlightenment, Ecumenism, Evangel: Theological Themes and Thinkers, 1550–2000*, edited by Alan P. F. Sell, 111–43. Studies in Christian History and Thought. Waynesboro, GA: Paternoster, 2005.

Bibliography

Sweeney, Douglas A. *Nathaniel Taylor, New Haven Theology, and the Legacy of Jonathan Edwards*. New York: Oxford University Press, 2005.
Tapper, Alan. "Priestley on Politics, Progress and Moral Theology." In *Enlightenment and Religion: Rational Dissent in Eighteenth-Century Britain*, edited by Knud Haakonssen, 272–86. Cambridge: Cambridge University Press, 1996.
Thompson, E. P. *The Making of the English Working Class*. London: Victor Gollancz, 1963.
Toulmin, Joshua. *The Practical Efficacy of the Unitarian Doctrine Considered, in a Series of Letters to the Rev. Andrew Fuller: Occasioned by His Publication Entitled "The Calvinist and Socinian Systems Examined and Compared, as to Their Moral Tendency."* 2nd ed. 1796. London: J. Johnson, 1801.
Walters, Kerry S. *The American Deists: Voices of Reason and Dissent in the Early Republic*. Lawrence: University Press of Kansas, 1992.
Watts, Michael R. *The Dissenters*. Vol. 1, *From the Reformation to the French Revolution*. Oxford: Clarendon, 1978.
White, Morton. *The Philosophy of the American Revolution*. New York: Oxford University Press, 1978.
Wills, Gary. *Inventing America: Jefferson's Declaration of Independence*. New York: Oxford University Press, 1979.
Wykes, David L. "Joshua Toulmin (1740–1815) of Taunton: Baptist Minister, Historian and Religious Radical." *The Baptist Quarterly* 39 (January 2002) 224–43.
Young, D. L. "The Place of Andrew Fuller in the Developing Modern Missions Movement." DPhil diss., Southwestern Baptist Theological Seminary, 1981.
Zagzebski, Linda T. *Virtues of the Mind: An Inquiry into the Nature of Virtue and the Ethical Foundations of Knowledge*. Cambridge: Cambridge University Press, 1996.

Name Index

Adam, 17, 39, 66
Adams, John, 21, 93
Aldridge, Owen, 20n69, 93
Anselm of Canterbury, 38–39
Apostle Paul, 79
Aristotle, 85
Ascol, Tom, 2n6, 93
Athanasius of Alexandria, 37–38
Augustine, Saint, 2, 38–39, 43, 64, 76–77, 93

Barbauld, Anna, 40
Basil of Caesarea, 38
Bebbington, D. W., 1–2, 93, 95
Bellamy, Joseph, 58, 95
Belsham, Thomas, 25, 27–29, 31, 36
Blount, Charles, 22
Bolingbroke, Lord, 31, 33, 40–41
Bowers, J.D, 17n45, 18n54, 93
Box, Bart, 2n6, 93
Brine, John, 9
Brooke, John H., 7, 16, 17n44, 18, 19n64, 93
Brewster, Paul, 1n2, 6n2, 93
Bunyan, John, 9
Burke, Edmund, 21–23, 31–32, 93, 95
Butler, Joseph, 37, 96

Calkin, Homer L., 21, 93
Calvin, John, 2, 38–39, 96

Carey, William, 12
Charry, Ellen, 3, 37–39, 69, 89, 93
Chun, Chris, 9–11, 43, 59, 94
Clipsham, E.F., 8, 37, 40, 94
Claeys, Gregory, 20n69, 94
Collins, Anthony, 31
Conway, Moncure Daniel, 20, 94, 97
Crisp, Oliver D., 58, 94–95
Crispus, 54–55

Daniel, Curt, 94
Diderot, Denis, 14

Edwards, John, 9
Edwards, Jonathan Jr., 58
Edwards, Jonathan, ix, xii, 2, 6, 8–12, 16, 34, 43–44, 46, 53, 58–59, 72–73, 94–96, 98
Eve, John, 7–8
Everts, W.W., 28n18, 94

Fiering, Norman, 34n55, 43n97, 94
Finn, Nathan A., 71n8, 94
Foner, Eric, 20n69, 94
Foster, Frank Hugh, 59n41, 94
Franklin, Benjamin, 21
Fruchtman, Jack, 20n69, 21n73, 94
Fuller, Andrew Gunton, xii, 6, 8, 35, 94–95
Fuller, Robert, 5

Name Index

Gaius, 54–55
Gerhard, John, 69
Gibbs, F.W., 17n45, 95
Gibbon, Edwards, 33
Gill, John, 9, 93, 95
Griffin, Rev. Mr., 46
Grotius, Hugo, 58
Gunton, Philippa, 5

Hall, Robert Sr., 8–9, 44
Harris, Ian, 21n74, 22, 23n80, 95
Haykin, Michael A.G., 1, 6n2, 8n15, 9n19 18n52, 26n3, 31n41, 32n48, 46n116, 59n41, 71n8, 94–97
Hiebert, Erwin N., 17n45, 95
Hopkins, Samuel, 58
Hoselton, Ryan P., 20n69, 95
Hume, David, 14–15, 33, 39, 41

Ivimey, Joseph, 1, 95

Jesus, 4, 24, 29–30, 34, 48, 62, 79, 80, 83–84
Jimack, Peter, 16, 95

Kant, Immanuel, 39
Keane, John, 20n69, 95
Kentish, John, 27, 29, 30–31, 36, 40, 96
Kirby, Arthur H., 1n6, 96
Kuklick, Bruce, 20n69, 96–97

Law, William, 37
Lindsey, Theophilus, 25
Locke, John, 14, 21, 38–39, 96
Lyons, James, 26

MacIntyre, Alisdair, 4, 15, 90–91, 96
May, Henry, 14, 18n57, 96
Marsden, George, 16n43, 53n20, 96
Mather, Cotton, 14
Mauldin, A. Chadwick, 2n6, 96
Morden, Peter, 2, 5n2, 11n28, 12n30, 96
Morris, J.W., 30n33, 96

Newton, Isaac, 14, 37
Noll, Mark, 1n4, 96
Nuttall, Geoffrey F., 1n3, 8n12, 97

Nettles, Tom, 1n3, 96

Oliver, Robert William, 2n6, 26n4, 97

Paine, Thomas, 3, 5, 14–16, 20–25, 32, 35, 40–41, 44, 48, 57, 61–62, 65, 74, 85, 88,-89, 93–97
Paley, William, 37
Pearce, Samuel, ix, 94
Plato, 85
Priestley, Jonas, 17
Priestley, Joseph, 3, 5, 13–20, 24–28, 34–35, 42, 44, 48, 52, 54, 57, 61, 75, 79, 88–89, 93, 95–98
Priestley, Mary, 17
Prochaska, Franklyn K., 32n47, 97

Rivers, Isabel, 97
Roberts, Phil, 1n3, 6n2, 97
Robinson, Robert, 26, 70, 74
Ryland, John Jr., 5–6, 8–9, 12–13, 25–28, 32, 35, 97

Schofield, Robert E., 17n45, 97
Sell, Alan P.F., 29n25, 31n44, 32n46, 36, 97
Shaftesbury, Earl of, 14, 41, 96
Socinus, Faustus, 29
Sweeney, Douglas A., 1n4, 59n41, 94–95, 98

Tapper, Alan, 17n45, 19n60, 98
Taylor, Abraham, 9
Thompson, E. P., 21n71, 98
Tindal, Matthew, 14, 23, 31, 33
Toland, John, 14, 31
Toulmin, Joshua, 27n9, 28–31, 36, 98

Voltaire, 14, 33

Walters, Kerry S., 20n69, 98
Watts, Michael R., 1n4, 18n55, 28n22, 98
West, Stephen, 58n41
White, Morton, 20n69, 21n71, 98
Whitefield, George, 26
Wilberforce, William, 31, 35, 87
Wills, Gary, 20n69, 98

Name Index

Wills, Gregory, xi
Wykes, David L., 28n23, 98

Young, D.L., 2n6, 98

Zagzebski, Linda T., 91n4, 98

Subject Index

aretegenic, vii, 3–4, 25, 37–39, 46–49, 51, 53–54, 58, 62, 66, 68–70, 80, 90
Arminianism, 9–11, 13, 17
atonement, 2, 18–20, 27–31, 46–48, 57–59, 61–65, 68–69, 78, 83, 89, 93–94

benevolence, 15, 43–44, 46, 77–78, 87, 89, 91
Bible, ix, 17, 22, 30, 32, 66–67, 73

Calvinism, 2–3, 6, 8–9, 14, 20, 29, 35, 46, 88–89, 94, 96–97
charity, 76, 78, 80, 84
Christ:
    deity/divinity of, 16, 18, 29, 30, 47, 63–64
    atonement of, 27–28, 30, 47, 61, 68
Christology, 26
conversion, 2–3, 7, 14, 18, 26

Daventry Academy, 17
disinterested love, 75–77, 87, 90
deism, 3–4, 9, 16, 20, 31–33, 35, 65, 89, 95, 97

Enlightenment, 2–5, 13–18, 20–21, 24–25, 33–34, 37–38, 50, 56–57, 59, 65, 67, 78–79, 85, 88, 90–91, 95–98

faith, 7–9, 11–12, 16–17, 39, 64, 68–69, 71–72, 80, 82, 84, 89, 91, 97

glory of God, 30, 48–49, 51–52, 72–73, 76, 83

happiness, 2, 4, 19, 23–24, 31, 35, 37, 39, 41–44, 46, 50–53, 67, 70–71, 73, 76–78, 81, 82–84, 87–89, 91
human depravity, 2, 29, 54–55, 69, 80
humility, 64, 78–80

inability:
    natural, 10–11, 15, 79, 88
    moral, vii, 4–5, 10–12, 15, 40, 68, 79, 88–89

knowledge, spiritual, 72–73, 77, 87, 90

love for God, 29, 43–46, 55–56, 66, 68, 70, 76–77, 87, 90
love of God, vii, 3–4, 7, 12–13, 24–25, 33, 35–37, 40, 42–46, 50–51, 55–58, 61, 65, 68–69, 75–78, 81–82, 84, 89–90

moral excellence, 2, 8, 12, 19, 24, 31, 49, 57–58, 66, 70, 75, 77, 89
moral law, 15, 42–43, 53, 55–56, 66, 68, 74, 86–87, 89

Subject Index

Northamptonshire Association, 11, 32

philosophy, 3, 15–21, 34, 39, 43, 67–69, 93–96, 98

Rational Dissent, 16–17, 75, 96, 98

Sandemanianism, 9, 70–72, 94–95
sapientia, 38–39, 69, 72, 89
scientia, 38, 40, 89

Scripture, 2, 9, 11, 17, 19, 23, 30–33, 35–36, 42, 45–48, 50, 53, 55, 62, 65, 66–69, 71, 75, 77–78, 85–86
self-love, 40, 44–46, 54–56, 64, 75, 90–91
Socinianism, 3–4, 9, 14, 18, 20, 25–26, 28–30, 35, 37, 42, 48, 50, 89, 96

The Modern Question, 1, 8–12, 97–98
Trinity, 2, 17–19, 23, 38, 46, 70
truth, 2, 4, 12, 18–19, 22–25, 27, 30, 32–40, 46–48, 51, 55, 57, 67, 69–72, 74–75, 77–78, 80–81, 87–91, 95

www.ingramcontent.com/pod-product-compliance
Lightning Source LLC
Chambersburg PA
CBHW070931160426
43193CB00011B/1652